Twice-Exceptional Boys:

A Roadmap to Getting it Right

Deborah J. Gennarelli

Gifted
UNLIMITED

Edited by: William D. Beuscher
Interior design: The Printed Page
Cover design: Kelly Crimi

Published by
Gifted Unlimited, LLC
12340 U.S. Highway 42, No. 453
Goshen, KY 40026
www.giftedunlimitedllc.com

ISBN: 978-1-953360-13-7

Dedication

To my courageous mother, Elizabeth, you inspired me to be the best daughter, wife, mother, and teacher possible.

To my husband, Bob, you bless me daily with your love and support.

To my smart and beautiful daughter, Nicole,
I am very proud of the woman you have become.

To my grandson, Milo, you stole my heart the day you were born.

Acknowledgments

First, I would like to thank Molly Isaacs-McLeod and Gifted Unlimited for seeing the importance of sharing information about 2e boys in a time when all types of gifted children are being overlooked.

Next, I must thank Jim Webb and Janet Gore. They recognized the meaningful work I was doing when I started writing about the twice-exceptional students I taught in my career.

I express my sincere gratitude to Gretchen Hirsch. I was blessed when she was put on my path to help shape my ideas in a book that shines. My experience working with Gretchen has been one of the highlights of my career.

I would like to thank the four special boys and families who allowed me to tell their stories in this book. Working with them through many twists and turns in their educational journeys has only deepened my commitment to support gifted children everywhere.

I would also like thank the classroom teachers I have worked with in my career who embraced learning about gifted children. They let go of myths and embraced the truths about smart kids. I saw lives change forever when this happened.

Finally, I must express my deepest appreciation to my husband for encouraging me to write about 2e boys. He understands my passion for gifted children, and he never let me doubt that I could turn the stories I always shared with others into a meaningful book.

Table of Contents

Preface **v**

Part 1: Introduction **1**

Chapter 1: Why Boys? **3**
Some General and Disturbing Facts About Boys' Schooling 3
Gifted Traits That Can Make School Difficult 4
Minority Gifted Boys 6
Boys' Early Problems in School 7
Special Issues for Gifted Boys 8
Societal Myths and Stereotypes About Boys 8
Androgyny in Gifted Boys 9
The Underachieving Gifted Boy 10

Chapter 2: What is Twice-Exceptionality? **11**
Definitions of Twice Exceptional, Gifted, and Learning Disabled 11
Categories of Twice Exceptional Children 16
Table 2.1. Types of Twice-Exceptional Individuals 17
Nontraditional Gifted Students 19
How Can We Identify Twice Exceptional Students? 21
The Planning Process for a Twice-Exceptional Child 22
Figure 2.1. Educational Team Planning 24
Figure 2.2. Twice-Exceptional Strategies 27

Chapter 3: Getting it Right: Teachers, Schools, and Parents **29**
Myths and Truths 29
Table 3.1. Examples of How to Differentiate a Lesson 31
Table 3.2. Specific Behaviors for Categories of Giftedness 36
Table 3.3. Types of Gifted Learners 43

Meeting Their Needs 46
A Strategy that Works: Cluster Grouping 47
How Can Parents Get It Right? Parenting Styles 48
Bold. 49
Authoritarian. 49
Permissive. 49
Overambitious. 50
Uninvolved 51
Table 3.4. Strategies to Promote Social and Emotional Development of Twice-Exceptional Children 51
Working for the Child 52

Part II: Four Gifted Boys: Mateo, Jamal, Melvin, and Jake 57

Chapter 4: Mateo's Story: Gifted with Marked Asynchronous Development and ADHD 59
Getting to Know My Student 59
Parenting Mateo 60
Attention Deficit Hyperactivity Disorder 64
Teaching Mateo 66
Kindergarten 66
First Grade 67
Asynchronous Development 68
The Importance of the Teacher 69
Second Grade 70
Third Grade 74
Table 4.1. Road Trip Assistance for Students Like Mateo 78

Chapter 5: Jamal's Story: Gifted with ADHD and Obsessive-Compulsive Disorder 83
Getting to Know My Student 83
Parenting Jamal 84
Attention Deficit Hyperactivity Disorder 85
Obsessive-Compulsive Disorder 86
Teaching Jamal 89
Second Grade 89
What We Learned 90
Time Management Strategies 91
Issues with Anxiety 93
Introversion 93

Table 5.1. Introverts and Extroverts 94
Third Grade 95
Table 5.2. Road Trip Assistance for Students like Jamal 99

Chapter 6: Melvin's Story: Gifted with Executive Function Disorder, Spatial Dysgraphia, and Speech Difficulties 103
Getting to Know My Student 103
Parenting Melvin 104
Teaching Melvin 106
First Grade 106
Second Grade 109
Organization Help 109
Executive Function Disorder 111
Third Grade 111
Dysgraphia 112
Single-Subject Acceleration 113
Fourth Grade 114
Table 6.1. Road Trip Assistance for Students like Melvin 117

Chapter 7: Jake's Story: Highly Gifted With A Language Learning Disability 121
Getting to Know My Student 121
Parenting Jake 122
Teaching Jake 124
Kindergarten 124
First Grade 125
Second Grade 126
Language Learning Disability 127
Third Grade 128
Fourth Grade 131
Mentors 134
A Big Question: To Whole-Grade Skip, or Not 136
7.1. Road Trip Assistance for Students like Jake 140

Part III: For Parents and Teachers 145

Chapter 8: Intervention Specialists: What They Do…and Why 147
A New Field 147
Washington's Attempts to Set Standards 148
Why So Few Gifted Interventionists? 152

Gifted Education by My State 154
Making the Right Decisions 156
What the Interventionist Does 158
The Conversations Must Continue 160

Chapter 9: Hints and Helps for Parents and Teaching 2e Boys 163
Emotional Intensity 163
Table 9.1. Strategies to Support Emotional Intensity in Gifted Boys 164
Hands-on-Learners 164
Table 9.2. Strategies to Support Hands-On Learning 166
Curiosity and Questioning 166
Table 9.3. Strategies to Support Questioning and Curiosity 167
Coping 167
Table 9.4. Strategies to Support Coping with Real Life 171

Epilogue 173

References 175

Endnotes 187

About the Author 195

Preface

Many years ago in my teaching career, I met a very smart seven-year-old boy who lit up a room when he entered it. His enthusiasm for learning was contagious. He could never just sit still and wait for his dozens of questions to be answered. This smart boy always went after the knowledge he sought with a passion. As the year progressed, I noticed that regular schoolwork became more frustrating and difficult for him. By the time this boy was ten years old, the shining light in his eyes had glossed over and turned to anger.

This student's story was the beginning of my journey to help and then write about twice-exceptional boys. Since then, I have worked with many, and along the way I documented the numerous twists and turns these students took as their teachers and parents tried to figure out reasons for their struggles in school. "Is he gifted?" "Does he have a learning disability?" "Should he see a pediatrician or a psychologist?" These were common questions often asked as part of an attempt to figure out what had happened to turn such engaging and happy children into students who seemed to hate coming to school.

As I began to do investigations of my own, I found myself asking questions like: 1) Are teachers and schools prepared to identify and work with gifted children? 2) Do educators understand that a gifted child can also have a learning disability? 3) Why is it so difficult for parents to find knowledgeable administrators and teachers who can help them find answers to their questions, and who can be part of the team that makes important educational decisions for their children? The answers I found were disheartening.

When I became a teacher more than thirty years ago, I wanted to make a positive difference in children's lives. People who are called to teach understand that the job is neither easy nor well paid. The rewards come when a child achieves all he or she is capable of and finds joy in learning. As I began my career in a regular classroom, I honed my teaching skills by working with many different types of students from kindergarten to fifth grade, and my classrooms included students from diverse socioeconomic backgrounds. Their classroom performance ranged from those who worked below grade level to children who were one or two years above grade level.

Year after year, I became increasingly aware that the smartest kids frequently were not sufficiently challenged in school. They often struggled to find a place where they could reach their fullest potential. In addition, many of the adults, both parents and teachers, had difficulty understanding or working with these bright but challenging children. I wanted to help this group of students, so I trained to become a gifted intervention specialist.

As I began my work with gifted children, I noticed some things that concerned me. First, I realized that many gifted students are not well-served in school, but I also came to realize that twice-exceptional boys faced special difficulties. These young boys, who had such high potential, entered school excited and happy, but soon found that their classrooms were not always places where they felt they fit in. They felt different than their classmates, and certain school tasks seemed particularly confusing and difficult for them. Within a year or so, they had become anxious, had developed behavior problems, and often were socially withdrawn and underachieving. They simply didn't fit the neat little boxes in which the adults expected them to operate. When these problems surfaced, teachers contacted me because they knew I championed this group of students, and parents were referred to me by counselors and administrators because they did not always have the answers to the questions parents asked.

As I worked closely with the adults to help these boys, I often used a simple analogy to get everyone on the same page. I compared a gifted child's journey to a family vacation. During the vacation, the family can either enjoy a trip filled with exciting learning opportunities and priceless memories, or they can suffer through various difficulties like unexpected curves and detours. The problems that occur are all caused by a lack of planning and leaving things to chance.

Gifted children may experience many twists, turns and detours in school because the planning needed for them has never been part of their educational path. They are expected to follow a typical and prescribed route, like the other children in their classes. However, sometimes their abilities cause certain activities to be very difficult for them, resulting in a rough road trip that is smooth for other children. Or they may prefer to take side roads that are of intense interest to them. Their personal GPS will not take them down a straight path-and often makes them a mystery to their parents, teachers, and administrators.

Outstanding educators begin every new school year making plans. During that period, a teacher may discover that he or she has been assigned one or more gifted students. If the educator has only minimal knowledge of gifted children and relies on the common myths about this group of students, these children will experience frustration and delays. A lack of preparation, planning and understanding will inevitably result in anxiety and unhappiness for both student and teacher, and it will be even more problematic if a child is twice-exceptional (2e)—that is, a child who is intellectually gifted but who also has a simultaneously existing disability, such as ADHD, autism spectrum disorder, or a learning disability in one or more areas (like dyslexia or dyscalculia). [1]

Parents also require guidelines to support and advocate for these special-needs children, and for working with teachers. They can help smooth their child's path by cooperating with schools. Sharing information about their child with teachers, such as identification of giftedness and/or learning disabilities, testing, and selection of appropriate curriculum, are essential. When parents are involved in these issues, they are better prepared to advocate effectively for their gifted children.

This book describes the school experiences of four twice-exceptional boys. They all began school without an educational plan. Soon after they had experienced only a small part of their educational journey, they found themselves lost and in need of help to reach their destination-or their highest potential.

What happens in schools to children who are 2e? Too often schools place their focus on the disability and ignore the giftedness. Because true abilities are not attended to, and such children are placed with other educationally disabled children, the gifted child loses the joy of learning. The light goes out of his eyes. While gifted girls are more likely to "dumb down" to fit in or withdraw into depression, particularly if they are 2e, (and some boys may do the same), more often the 2e boys develop behavior problems where they act out, dramatically underachieve, and engage in risky behaviors because they are frustrated and angry that their learning is stymied.[2] Some of these very bright young men may even end up in the juvenile justice system, definitely the wrong environment for them.

I worked with each of the four boys you will read about over long periods of time. I also worked with their parents and teachers. Their educational paths were full of difficult detours, but each boy was able to get back on track after changes took place in home and school. It is my hope that readers will learn from these stories how to work with schools and families to steer their own children to the most productive educational path.

At the end of each boy's story is an important "road trip assistance" table that outlines roadblocks (problems experienced in school), road maps (possible solutions to the problems), and destinations (accomplishment of educational balance and dynamics for students). Teachers and parents must decide the paths that work best for each child as they help struggling students reach their potential. One should not assume that every step in the table is implemented for every child regardless of their twice-exceptionality.

Finally, the last chapter in this book includes some very helpful guidelines and suggestions for parents and teachers. You may choose to start there before reading each boy's story. Understanding emotional intensity, hands on learning, the expressions of curiosity, coping skills, and the roles of these dynamics in 2e boys' lives, will help you plan the best route to take while helping each student reach their full potential and live a happier life.

Part 1:
Introduction

Chapter 1
Why Boys?

As schools in the United States have swung toward an emphasis on science, technology, engineering, and math (STEM) education, the educational literature has taken a swing toward gender fairness as it relates to these fields.[3] Recent discussions include the fact that girls and women are underrepresented in STEM advanced coursework, college degree programs and careers. Because the discussions often focus on the reasons girls are excluded-or why they sometimes exclude themselves from these endeavors-boys are rarely mentioned. The focus on girls has taken attention away from the fact that boys are experiencing equally troubling issues in school, sometimes more so than girls.[4]

Some General and Disturbing Facts About Boys' Schooling

Below are some general and disturbing facts about the status of boys' schooling:

As reported in the 2019 Digest of Education Statistics by the National Center for Education, boys:

- Were more likely to receive an out-of-school suspension.
- Were expelled 2 ½ times more than girls.
- Were more likely to use illicit drugs.
- Were twice as likely to be in a fight at school.[5]

These inequalities also cross racial boundaries, and appear to be even more dramatic for minority boys. The same center reported in 2019 that:

- Black boys were threatened or injured with a weapon at school more often than white boys.
- Twice as many Black boys were expelled from school as compared to white boys.[6]

Gifted Traits That Can Make School Difficult

Of course, all boys and girls have challenges growing up, but this is particularly true of gifted students. Gifted children of whatever sex tend to exhibit certain traits that can make for successful learning, but at the same time those traits may make their school experience more difficult.[7] For example, gifted children, both boys and girls:

- *Are intense.* This is perhaps the number one hallmark of gifted students both in their feelings and often in their behaviors. They experience feelings more keenly; that is, they experience emotions like happiness, sadness, shame, embarrassment, and achievement more deeply than typical students. Classrooms are often the place where these feelings come to the forefront-and those moments can be either joyous or miserable.
- *Are voraciously curious and questioning.* This is a laudable quality, but it can become a problem if the child's interest does not match that of the teacher and the child is disruptive in the classroom, interrupting the teacher and other students because he has a burning question. A gifted child may be strong-willed, push the limits, and even be oppositional.
- *May be perfectionists.* Gifted children sometimes melt down if they don't get a perfect grade because they see only two possibilities: either perfect, or failure. And failure (even if the score is 98) is intolerable to them. As the author Lisa Van Gemert has said, such children have difficulties learning to accept "good enough."[8]

- *Are original thinkers.* Most teachers will value this creative kind of thinking, but some will not because it doesn't fit the mold, and they don't know how to accommodate it, let alone grade it.
- *Have immense energy.* This kind of vitality can make them classroom stars, but it also can result in problems arising from their pent-up physical and mental energy. Children's classrooms are often places where they are expected to sit still and absorb what the teacher is saying. Some of these children are unable to sleep because they can't turn off their minds, and subsequently come to class fatigued. These students (all students, in fact) must be permitted to move physically or the extra 'gifted' energy can come out as frustration, anger, and rudeness.
- *Have an unusual sense of humor.* A student's sense of humor lightens the mood of the classroom, but when he becomes the class clown, it can be obnoxious and get in the way of everyone's learning.
- *Have a varying attention span.* When the child is bored because the class is again going over what he has known since the year before, his attention wanders and he is likely to be "off task." However, when he's engaged in a topic or activity that interests him, it can be hard to pry him away from a project when the class is moving on to a different activity.
- *May be highly empathetic and sensitive.* Gifted students may also worry inordinately about fairness, in the classroom as well as the world, about such issues as famine, war, school shootings, and other things they cannot control. This can create much anxiety that hinders them and may result in them being children who struggle in school.
- *Have abilities that may not be uniform across areas.* A common belief is that if you have high ability in one area, you are likely to have equal abilities in other areas. In fact, the brighter the child, the more likely it is for the child's abilities to vary-often dramatically. A child may be gifted in one or more areas but have other abilities that are average or even below average.

> Some children might be gifted and Learning Disabled (LD), or gifted with Attention Deficit Disorder (ADD), or Obsessive-Compulsive Disorder (OCD), etc.

Children's attitudes towards learning significantly affect their decisions to pursue further education as well as their career choices. If a student reaches middle school and he has not experienced education as a fulfilling journey, he is likely to be at risk of not pursuing a college degree, or worse, he may drop out of high school altogether. The children dropping out may very well be unidentified gifted students-those who have the brain power to make real changes in the world-and their loss is a tragedy.[9]

Minority Gifted Boys

Boys from minority and low-income backgrounds are underrepresented in gifted education and over-represented in special education.[10] According to the Coalition of Schools Educating Boys of Color (COSEBOC), some high-minority and high-poverty schools hesitate to provide resources for gifted coursework because of a widely held belief that there are insufficient students in these schools to warrant the course offerings. Many low-income and minority children are never even tested for giftedness. Therefore, many students with high intelligence and abilities go undiscovered.[11]

Adding to this dilemma, each minority group has its own conceptions of giftedness and the purposes of education. Psychologists Barbara Kerr and Sanford Cohn write in their book *Smart Boys* about their experiences working with talented boys from many ethnic backgrounds through counseling workshops and special projects. They found many Black boys live in urban areas where they face issues of poverty, violence, and poor schools.[12] They are often living in survival mode; daily food, safety, clothing, and shelter are more important than getting good grades in school. Their schooling is likely to suffer because they are stereotyped as overachievers; if students excel only in math and science their general creative efforts often are overlooked.[13]

Hispanic boys suffer because they sometimes mask their talents due to language barriers or they struggle with traditional male roles that conflict with their own intellectual and personal values.[14] Finally,

Native-American boys strongly rooted in their communities and traditions may reject opportunities to advance because this threatens their connection to the communities, the land, and the people they love.[15] Without interventions, including identification of smart boys of all races, the achievement gap between whites and minority students will continue to increase.

Boys' Early Problems in School

Boys' problems begin quite early. In *Trouble with Boys*, education journalist Peg Tyre reported that preschool boys were nearly five times more likely to be expelled than girls.[16] Some of these expulsions probably were due to typical "young boy behavior" such as high energy and poor impulse control. Though she did not specify what percentage of these boys were gifted, it is likely to be three to five percent, which is the percentage thought of as gifted in the general population. Many preschools today, rather than letting children learn by doing and allowing abundant free play, now concentrate on scholastic tasks requiring students to sit and be quiet for long periods of time. This is antithetical to the way many boys (people!) learn. Their natural behavior is to move around and explore. Yet in many schools, if they can't control themselves in a restricted environment, expulsion may follow.

Young boys are also less developed than girls in fine motor skills, coping mechanisms, and verbal ability.[17] They may have more difficulty holding a pencil or turning a book's page when compared to the girls in their class.

In the book *Boys and Girls Learn Differently*, author Michael Gurian explains brain-based differences that affect boys and girls. For example, in children ages 4-6, girls are better at fine motor skills and coordination of fine motor tasks, whereas boys are better at solving math problems without talking.[18] If the child is forced to master a skill before he is ready, he is likely to misbehave as an expression of his feelings of frustration.

Special Issues for Gifted Boys

Given the difficulties mentioned above, it is perhaps not surprising that the National Center for Education Statistics data shows that among six-year-old to twenty-one-year-old students enrolled in public schools in 2019, a higher percentage of males (18%) than females (10%) received special education services under the Individuals with Disabilities Education Act (IDEA).[19] This includes Attention Deficit Hyperactivity Disorder, which can be determined to be a disability under IDEA as "Other Health Impairment." Although some boys show behaviors that suggest the diagnosis, ADHD is also frequently a wrong diagnosis. In *Misdiagnosis and Dual Diagnoses of Gifted Children and Adults*, James T. Webb et al explain that behaviors typical for the gifted may be mistaken for behavioral disorders in more than twenty-five percent of gifted students.[20] Though some of these children may have ADHD, many of these children are simply behaving in reaction to an inappropriate educational placement, intolerance of their advanced abilities, or parenting that doesn't recognize or understand the child's giftedness.

Societal Myths and Stereotypes About Boys

Author William Pollock, Ph.D., investigates three myths about boys that are deeply embedded in our culture. These societal myths keep gifted boys from expressing their true selves and have a profound impact on their educations and futures. The myths include:

- "Boys will be boys." That is, boys' testosterone will cause them to be emotionally unaware and aggressive.
- "Boys *should* be boys." They must fulfill the stereotypes of the dominant male and never act "like a girl."
- Boys are toxic. A boy's childhood exploratory play may erroneously be confused with adult predatory behavior.[21]

The truth is that boys' behavior is shaped more by their family, positive mentorships and loved ones than by nature.[22] Certainly, boys can be-and often are-empathetic, kind, generous, and polite, and there are many different ways of being male in our society. In fact, societal expectations are changing. It is far more acceptable now for boys to be androgynous, gender fluid, gay, transgender, or unsure of their gender identify.[23]

The male myths and stereotypes in our culture force boys to seek ways to be masculine. Because society has constructed and often stereotyped what a man should be and how he should act (manly, athletic, brave, strong), gifted boys with special sensitivities and talents often suppress these skills to maintain a masculine façade. Some gifted boys conform to the ideal of the rugged athlete even when they don't like sports. In a keynote speech titled "Gender and Genius" at The College of William and Mary, psychologist Barbara Kerr stated, "Gifted boys learn very early that if they are smart, they had better be smart and athletic, as athletic ability makes intelligence acceptable".[24] If they live in environments that do not value academics or artistic achievements, the boy will likely experience high levels of stress trying to please parents, teachers, coaches, and peers. Eventually, some gifted boys "resent the fact that their intensity cannot be directed toward intellectual or creative activities if they are to prove they are *real boys*."[25]

Androgyny in Gifted Boys

Many highly gifted and creative children tend to show more androgynous traits than average students.[26] Androgyny is the combination of traditionally masculine and feminine interests and behaviors. And gifted youngsters, particularly those who are highly gifted, are more likely to show such a mix of interests.[27] Since androgyny is generally more accepted in girls, boys must often cope with the psychological (as compared with aesthetically visual) androgyny that exists in highly gifted and creative individuals. Androgyny does not mean that these students are gay, but simply that they are more in tune with both masculine and feminine strengths. A boy may be an athlete, but may also love baking, which is considered by most to be a feminine domain, or he may enjoy NASCAR racing, but also have a tender heart that is easily moved to tears. He is no less a boy for displaying these traits.

These more androgynous boys can become targets for bullies and face intense name-calling and physical violence because they live outside the boy code.[28] Many prominent researchers in androgyny and gender studies have noted that psychological androgyny has important beneficial consequences, particularly that androgyny can expand the range of behaviors available to everyone.[29] Ultimately, parents and teachers of boys who express a desire to cook, paint, write poetry, design clothes, or become a nurse should encourage them to embrace this side of their personality. These boys should not feel diminished as males. Maleness, after all, is not defined by what they do, but by who they are. Boys with androgynous characteristics should be celebrated.

The Underachieving Gifted Boy

Underachievement, a term used to describe the discrepancy between a student's performance and his or her potential or ability to perform at a much higher level,[30] has a variety of causes.[31] The child may be bored because he already knows what's being taught, or perhaps more significantly, he is facing an unexpected challenge. Most young, gifted children in the early grades don't have to study much because they are already so far ahead of age mates. When they are finally confronted with assignments that challenge them, they may struggle because they lack persistence, resilience, or good study habits, or because they have a learning disability that has not yet been recognized. Because they are suddenly challenged and have trouble understanding the work they are to do, they might procrastinate or "forget" to turn in assignments. They may become depressed or even defiant, not because they have lost their gifts, but because they're afraid of failing or of telling a teacher they don't understand the assignment.

In some cases, a student may fail to achieve his potential because he doesn't want to stand out or be different from his peers. He may hide his intelligence or talent to fit in.

Some underachieving boys, though, don't make the grade because they are twice-exceptional, or 2e for short. They have a hidden learning disability such as dyslexia, dysgraphia, dyscalculia, sensory processing issues, executive function disorders, or another academically handicapping condition. Low grades and negative feedback result in their developing low expectations for themselves. A boy may become angry, anxious, or depressed. He may even engage in antisocial behaviors.

Once the disability is uncovered, schools will often pay attention only to the handicapping condition and rarely consider that the child might be gifted as well.

In a powerful article by a mother and her 2e son, -*Through His Eyes and Through His Mother's Eyes*—authors Joseph and his mother Holly Hughes point to early challenges Joseph faced that lasted until high school. Joseph described his school experience saying, "It's like the square-peg-in-the-round-hole, only worse. I'm a triangle and the only way to fit into that round hole is to shave off all my edges and shrink a lot." Holly describes the experience of trying to help her son battle his challenges in school saying, "I had a need to understand how I could help make life less painful for him. I considered every route on the map without ever knowing that I was on the wrong map!"[32]

Joseph represents the thousands of smart boys in our schools who constantly struggle to reach their potential. His mother represents the thousands of parents looking for answers to their son's problems. Despite the enormous progress made in ensuring equal educational opportunities for girls since the passing of Title IX in 1972, the United States Department of Education confirms that "much work remains to be done if we are to achieve full gender equity among our nation's students." [33] Because girls and young women account for the majority of students attending American colleges and universities,[34] we need to remind ourselves of all the factors working against boys in schools and society. There is no easy solution to fix a problem that has escalated for decades, but we must work to give each child a fighting chance to achieve success and satisfaction in their learning.

Twice-exceptional boys face an extra hurdle in school. They show a pattern of extreme strengths combined with areas of significant difficulty. They are among the most frequently under-identified population in our schools. According to the National Education Association, parents and teachers should consider the following when identifying a twice-exceptional student.[35]

- Use multiple data sources for gifted programming identification: intelligence and achievement tests, teacher reports, creativity tests, student interviews, and student work portfolios.

- Avoid combining multiple pieces of data into a single score because combining scores allows lower scores to depress the total score, thereby disqualifying students with strengths for gifted programs.
- Compare expected performance on statewide standardized testing as well as psychological educational assessments, with actual performance using the student's daily classroom achievement, as well as other authentic assessments.
- Be aware that identification of giftedness is seldom pursued for a student whose gifts and disabilities mask one another. As such, be hyper-vigilant about looking for subtle indicators of exceptionality in students.
- Use culturally sensitive assessment processes to prevent language and cultural differences from creating bias in the identification process.

We owe it to these children to actively seek and identify them, because myths and lack of understanding often cause us to miss them. Then we need to provide encouraging and functional challenges for their giftedness as well as remediation for their disability.[36]

Chapter 2
What is Twice-Exceptionality?

I cannot count the number of times I have been asked by parents, teachers, and administrators if a student really could be gifted and also have a learning disability. The answer is yes, and these students are truly twice-exceptional (2e). Due to their individual strengths and weaknesses, they have unique and often quite challenging educational needs.

Definitions of Twice Exceptional, Gifted, and Learning Disabled

No federal definition covers 2e students. However, the Joint Commission on Twice-Exceptional Students, representing The National Research Center on the Gifted and Talented (2009), described 2e learners as:

> *Students who give evidence of the potential for high achievement capability in areas such as specific academics, general intellectual ability, creativity, leadership, and/or visual, spatial, or performing arts, AND also give evidence of one or more disabilities as defined by federal or state eligibility criteria such as specific learning disabilities; speech and language disorders, emotional/behavioral disorders, physical disabilities, autism spectrum, or other impairments such as attention deficit hyperactivity disorder (ADHD).*[37]

It is unfortunate we don't know how many 2e children are in our schools because so many of them are never formally identified. However, it is thought to be approximately 2-5% of the student population.[38] In classrooms, these children are most commonly noticed for what they cannot do, not for a specific talent they may demonstrate. Susan Baum, Director of the National Institute for 2e Research and Development and author of *To Be Gifted and Learning Disabled* suggests we must first have a good understanding of both the terms gifted and learning disabled before we can truly help the 2e student.[39] School districts typically use state recognized definitions of educational terms to provide a framework for programs and services, but because serving gifted children is not mandated by the federal government, nearly every state has its own definition of gifted and talented.

Most states define giftedness based on a comparison to others of the same age. According to the National Association for Gifted Children's *State of the States in Gifted Education Policy and Practice Data* (2019), thirty-two states require multiple education criteria to identify gifted students. The most frequently used data include IQ scores, achievement test scores, parent/teacher referrals, a range of state approved assessments, and student performance portfolios.[40] This report also notes that most school districts follow their state definition of *gifted,* but it is not mandated. This lack of a common definition makes it difficult to identify gifted children in America. Regardless of state or district definitions, many educators and parents look to the National Association for Gifted Children for a clear meaning of giftedness. It states:

> *Students with gifts and talents perform—or have the capability to perform—at higher levels compared to others of the same age, experience, and environment in one or more domains. They require modification(s) to their educational experience(s) to learn and realize their potential. Student with gifts and talents:*
>
> - *Come from all racial, ethnic, and cultural populations, as well as all economic strata.*
> - *Require sufficient access to appropriate learning opportunities to realize their potential.*
> - *Can have learning and processing disorders that require specialized intervention and accommodation.*

- *Need support and guidance to develop socially and emotionally as well as in their areas of talent.*
- *Require varied services based on their changing needs.*[41]

It is important for parents and teachers to understand the hallmark characteristic of giftedness is asynchronous development. This means a mismatch between the cognitive, emotional, and physical development of gifted individuals. In children, this can be observed as uneven development across skill levels. For example, a second-grade child may read at a fifth-grade level, but he may work at grade level or even below in writing. I have observed a very gifted third grader discuss the International Space Station in detail, but he constantly got his feelings hurt over things that did not bother his classmates. His cognitive and emotional development were out of sync. Asynchronous development is more pronounced for twice-exceptional students.[42]

Although gifted children may have similar IQ scores, they may not have similar skills, rates of development, abilities, and interests. They can become frustrated when they observe those around them and realize they cannot accomplish some things as well as others. Individuals who work with gifted children should be aware of asynchronous development before making referrals for a possible learning disability or behavioral disorder. Too often misdiagnoses are made because of misunderstanding the child.[43]

In 1975, the U.S. government signed into law the Individuals with Disabilities Education Act (IDEA). This act has been amended many times, but its purpose has not changed. IDEA protects the rights of children with disabilities and gives parents a voice in their child's education. It requires schools to identify students who require special education programs and services. A learning disability is recognized as a

> *"...disorder in one or more of the basic psychological processes involved in understanding or in using language, spoken or written, that may manifest itself in the imperfect ability to listen, think, speak, read, write, spell, or to do mathematical calculations."*[44]

Not every child with learning and attention issues is eligible for special education services under IDEA. First, a child must be found to have at least one of the thirteen kinds of disabilities including:

- Autism
- Deaf-blindness
- Hearing impairment/deafness
- Visual impairment, including blindness
- Emotional disturbance
- Intellectual disability
- Orthopedic impairment
- Other health impairment (including ADHD)
- Specific learning disability (including dyslexia, dyscalculia, and dysgraphia, among others)
- Speech or language impairment
- Traumatic brain injury
- Multiple disabilities[45]

Categories of Twice Exceptional Children

Twice-exceptional children may be found in one of the following three categories if the student: [46]

- May be formally identified as gifted, but not have an identified disability. That is, the child's giftedness masks the disability.
- May be formally identified as having a disability, but not identified as gifted. In other words, the disability has concealed the giftedness.
- The student may not be formally identified as either gifted or disabled because the components hide one another. To teachers and parents, neither giftedness nor the disability is evident.

The National Education Association advises those who work with children to take a closer look at the types of twice-exceptionality, and to recognize that 2e children can become successful adults. The following chart includes specific areas of disability recognized under IDEA, examples of disabilities for each area, and successful people identified as gifted with a learning disability. The list should provide hope for parents, teachers, and students. Twice-exceptionality may be a hurdle, but it does not need to be a barrier to success. The key is to address both the disability and the giftedness in the child's education plan.

Table 2.1. Types of Twice-Exceptional Individuals

Area of Disability	Examples of Disabilities	Successful 2e Individuals
Physical Disability	• Tourette syndrome • Paralysis • ALS • Muscular dystrophy • Cerebral palsy • Chronic or acute health problem such as a heart condition	• Steven Hawkins, Jacob Javits (ALS) • Franklin D. Roosevelt (Paralysis) • Paula Abdul, Toni Braxton, Nick Cannon, Selena Gomez (Lupus) • Shawn White (Tetralogy of Fallot) • Larry Byrd, Barry Manilow (Atrial fibrillation)
Sensory Disability	• Deaf/hearing impaired • Blindness	• Ludwig von Beethoven, Jim Kyte, Marlee Matlin (Deaf) • Steven Colbert, Thomas Edison (Hearing impairment) • Andrea Bocelli, Ray Charles, Jose Feliciano, Governor David Paterson, Marla Runyan, Erik Weihenmayer, Stevie Wonder (Blind) • Helen Keller (Deaf and blind)

Area of Disability	Examples of Disabilities	Successful 2e Individuals
Deficit in Social Functioning	• Autism Spectrum Disorder	• Dr. Temple Grandin, (Autism) • Dan Aykroyd, Susan Boyle, Daryl Hannah (Asperger syndrome)
Emotional and/or Behavioral Disorders	• Schizophrenia • Depression • Anxiety • Bipolar disorder • Obsessive compulsive disorder	• Winton Churchill, Sheryl Crow, Abraham Lincoln, J. K. Rowling (Depression) • Patty Duke, Demi Lovato, Jane Pauley, Jean-Claude Van Damme, Catherine Zeta Jones (Bipolar disorder) • John Nash, Jr. (Schizophrenia) • Justine Timberlake (OCD/ ADHD) • Howie Mandel (ADHD/ depression/OCD) • David Beckham, Cameron Diaz, Howard Hughes, Steve Jobs (OCD)
Brain-Based Impairments	• ADHD • Executive function disorder	• Terry Bradshaw, Jim Carrey, James Carville, Scott Kelly, Adam Levine, Lisa Ling, David Neeleman, Ty Pennington, Michael Phelps, Will Smith (ADHD) • Richard Branson, Channing Tatum, Vince Vaughn (ADD/ dyslexia)

Area of Disability	Examples of Disabilities	Successful 2e Individuals
Specific Learning Disabilities	• Dyslexia • Dysgraphia • Dyscalculia • Sensory deficit disorder	• Cher, Anderson Cooper, Tom Cruise, Richard Engel, Whoopi Goldberg, Tommy Hilfiger, Keira Knightley, Jay Leno, Keanu Reeves, Charles Schwab, Steven Spielberg, Tim Tebow, Henry Winkler (Dyslexia)
Speech-Language	• Stuttering • Impaired articulation • Voice impairment	• Joe Biden, Emily Blunt, Samuel L. Jackson, James Earl Jones, Byron Pitts, Carly Simon, Bruce Willis, Lewis Carroll (Stuttering) • B.B. King (Stuttering/ diabetes)
Other Health Impairments	• Diabetes • Epilepsy	• Nick Jonas, Patti LaBelle, George Lucas, Bret Michaels, Mary Tyler Moore, Jean Smart, Sonia Sotomayor (Type 1 diabetes)

Nontraditional Gifted Students

Far too many nontraditional gifted students, such as recent immigrants, children living in poverty or those with physical challenges, are underrepresented in advanced programs. A study by the U.S. Department of Education's Office for Civil Rights concluded only one percent of students who received IDEA ('disability') services are in gifted and talented education programs, compared with seven percent of their general education peers.[47] Even when students are identified as 2e, many schools feel uncomfortable accommodating both of the child's learning needs. Sometimes it appears we are asking these students to choose one or the other: *Are you learning disabled or gifted?* Of course, it is quite possible to be both gifted and alternately abled, and the goal is to support all of this dynamic.

Under IDEA, twice exceptional students *should* be accommodated and supported. However, there is no specific language in the law regarding these students. Even after the Department of Education issued a memorandum to special education leaders in 2015 clarifying the federal government's position regarding the evaluation and provision of special education services to 2e students, problems still exist.[48]

Schools sometimes argue that if a student's achievements are commensurate with the average for his or her age level, a disability does not exist. Also, if a smart student is identified with a learning disability, a school may decide not to adjust advanced classes or programs to work with the special needs of that gifted student. This forces the student to take lower-level courses and holds him back from his highest level of accomplishment. It is important to remember that twice-exceptional students require both advanced programming for their giftedness and accommodations for their learning disability.

Although the Gifted and Talented Education Act, known informally as the Javits Act, as well as IDEA shine a light on special populations of students, these government regulations are not enough to ensure that 2e children are supported individually. A collaborative effort among classroom teachers, special education teachers, gifted specialists, and parents is needed to identify 2e students early so interventionists can be applied, and so that students don't struggle for years with increasingly widening learning gaps.

If twice-exceptional students are ignored, it is almost certain that frustration will escalate and take the form of poor study and work skills, underachievement, carelessness, acting out, or even aggression towards peers and adults. Teachers often find 2e children are disruptive in their classrooms. Susan Winebrenner, a well-known expert in classroom accommodations for the gifted, writes, "These students can be off task, acting out, daydreaming, or complaining about their frustrations. Teachers are caught between belief and disbelief, as they wonder if the student can do a task or is simply *too lazy* to exert the required effort to complete their work."[49] Despite the frustration teachers and parents might experience with 2e children, progress is possible when school and home environments are nurturing.

How Can We Identify Twice Exceptional Students?

Identifying a 2e child can be difficult. One reason is because there are many combinations of 2e. First, there are varieties of giftedness, such as intellectual (IQ 130+), academic (math, science, language arts), artistic (art, music, dance), kinesthetic (athletic), as well as verbal, visual-spatial, and problem-solving abilities. There are also the common learning disabilities, such as dyslexia (reading), dysgraphia (writing), dyscalculia (math), and processing disorders (sensory-visual-auditory), language disorder (problems using and understanding spoken and/or written language), speech disability, ADHD (poor attention and executive functions), and emotional disorders (depression, bipolarity, anxiety, OCD).

Adults who recognize a decline in a child's school performance and a child's growing frustration should look for the cause. After things like poor eyesight, hearing, or other physical problems are ruled out, teacher and parent should seek screening to determine the cause of the child's problem. When a child shows a particular strength or strengths (like completing difficult puzzles or solving advanced math problems) but also shows significant struggles in other areas, it is time for parents and teachers to seek further advice from trained professionals, like a school psychologist, a gifted intervention specialist in the school district, or perhaps a pediatric neuropsychologist, and to convey their observations to these relevant professionals. These individuals can help sort out the difficulties and can help plan for the child's education needs. This planning often includes individual tests (rather than group tests) for giftedness. Ability testing may include: the WISC-IV, Stanford Binet, Woodcock Johnson, and the Naglieri Nonverbal Test (effective for students from culturally and linguistically different or low-income backgrounds to eliminate barriers). They are recommended by the National Association for Gifted Children.[50] Individual tests for determining achievement level may include the Peabody Individual Achievement Test, the Wide Range Achievement Test, The Woodcock-Johnson Achievement Tests, or others. Some parents seek advice from their child's pediatrician, who may direct them to a neuropsychologist or other diagnostician who tests for giftedness and learning disabilities. Pediatric neuropsychologists administer additional specialized tests, depending on what original tests have been given in school and the child's behavior suggest.[51]

Parents can also contact their state department of education or state gifted association to find professionals who work with families of gifted children. Associate Director of Denver's Gifted Development Center, Barbara Gilman, says, "Professional testing ensures maximum expertise in interpreting results and providing helpful recommendations."[52] I have worked with many families who have found clarity after thorough testing was completed by a trained professional. If parents choose such professional testing, they must get detailed explanations of all the results so they can speak intelligently to school personnel when important educational decisions are made for their child.

Parents may balk at having to take their child to a neuropsychologist for testing because of the expense. A complete battery of tests can cost around $2000. But this testing is valuable, particularly when it shows details about how the child learns best, and what areas are weak and need remediation or help. For example, often there are exercises that a child with dyslexia or dysgraphia can undertake to improve reading or math skills. After testing is completed, parents will have a written report summarizing results and recommendations for school support. The psychologist may visit the school and attend a meeting with teachers about the child. Keep in mind that if the child is dealing with a disability, a parent may request an IEE (Independent Education Evaluation), which typically is at school expense. In such cases, it is best to seek advice from a Special Education advocate or attorney in one's state to satisfy procedural requirements for payment.

The Planning Process for a Twice-Exceptional Child

When a 2e student is identified, the problem-solving team at school, including the gifted specialist and special education interventionist, will begin the process of planning for the student's special needs. The planning by the Intervention Assistance Team attempts to:

- *Identify the student's strengths and interests.* Support and success with a student's strengths gives the student a strong self-concept and a sense of self-efficacy. Instruction that builds on students' interests can motivate them to persevere when they feel challenged.

- *Identify the student's challenges and educational needs by examining existing data collected by teachers and parents.* These challenges could be a weak content area, such as reading; or they could be behavioral concerns.
- *Create an action plan by selecting one strength area and one challenge area as the focus.* The action plan should include measurable goals, interventions, materials, and necessary accommodations and/or modifications. The Intervention Assistance Team (IAT)—also called Response to Intervention Team, School-Based Intervention Team, etc.—carefully monitor the student's growth and the overall success of the plan and should schedule regular follow-up meetings to assess the student's progress.

Identifying and supporting twice-exceptional students is often a low priority in schools, but the benefit to the 2e students is significant. When teachers and parents empower these children by identifying and working with their talents and strengths, they build the students' self-confidence. Confidence in their own abilities is essential when 2e students experience problems, whether at school or at home. Changing negative attitudes to positive ones can have a profound impact on 2e students' achievements throughout their lives.[53]

How to do this will vary from student to student, and the planning and interventions can be challenging and require focus at home as well as at school. Here is an example.

Figure 2.1. Educational Team Planning[54]

Student Ricardo

Ricardo is a third grade 2e boy who has many strengths. He is an advanced reader who can locate information in books quickly and uses advanced vocabulary. Ricardo enjoys being creative and is described as an original thinker. He likes to listen to music and learns easily when music is involved in the learning process.

Ricardo also has some significant challenges in school. He has difficulty following multistep routines, completes few tasks or projects, and is a poor writer. He has difficulty making friends because he annoys others. He has a very difficult time recovering from stressful school situations.

Grade 3

S-Student Strength C-Student Challenge	Specific Strengths	Specific Challenges/ Concerns
Cognitive Processing S Visual Processing _Auditory Processing C Sequential Processing _Conceptual Processing _Processing Speed _Attention _Memory _Executive Functioning _Other	• Remembers what he has read • Can locate a specific piece of information in a book • Very good speller	• Mixes up what comes first, next, last • Difficulty following through on multistep routines • Sustained attention and follow through

S-Student Strength C-Student Challenge	Specific Strengths	Specific Challenges/ Concerns
Specific Academic S Reading S Reading Fluency C Writing C Writing Fluency _Math _Math Fluency _Science _Social Studies _Other	• Reads and comprehends at sixth-grade level • Reads test quickly and with expression • Advanced vocabulary	• Difficulty putting ideas together • Poor narrative sequencing • Mental fatigue when writing
Creativity S Creative Thinking S Creative Productivity _Creative Problem Solving _Risk Taking _Other	• Overflows with ideas • Prefers company of other creative children • Enjoys creating new ways to do routine tasks • Original thoughts	• Creative endeavors take time away from other classroom assignments • Not motivated by grades • Self-Critical • Frustration caused by intensity • Requires extra time to complete projects
Visual, Spatial, Performing Arts _Visual Perception _Spatial Perception S Musical/Rhythmic _Bodily/Kinesthetic _Other	• Shows sensitivity to rhythm, melodies, and sounds • Enjoys music playing in the background when working • Learns easily when information is sung or tapped out in rhythm (math facts)	

S-Student Strength C-Student Challenge	Specific Strengths	Specific Challenges/ Concerns
Physical/Psychomotor _Sensory Integration _Hearing _Vision C ADD/ADHD _Bodily		• Restless • Focus is only on self • Few tasks or goals are achieved
Interpersonal/ Leadership S Communicating C Understanding Others C Peer Relations _Self-Advocacy _Other	• Advanced vocabulary • Able to clearly express his or her own thoughts, ideas, and opinions • Active listener	• Little interaction during unstructured time • Difficulty making friends
Intrapersonal/Social Emotional _Understanding Self _Introspection/ Reflection C Resiliency C Coping _Behavioral Issues _Perfectionism		• Negative internal dialogue • Requires use of a "stress ball" most of the day • Anxieties produce physical ailments • Difficulty recovering from stressful school situations

Here are some customized educational strategies suggested for this 2e boy:

Figure 2.2. Twice-Exceptional Strategies

Example

Name: Ricardo

Grade: Third

School: Apple Elementary

Date: May 2020

Learning Style Observation		
• Strengths • Advanced reading ability • Creative thinker	• Interests • Music • Video games • Non-fiction topics (weather, animals)	• Challenges • Writing • Incomplete assignments

Strength/Interest-Based Accommodations

- Use flexible, non-permanent instructional grouping practices designed to facilitate accelerated/advanced academic learning (cluster grouping, cross-age grouping, interest groups).[55]
- Use challenging reading programs/materials (e.g., Junior Great Books).
- Provide high-level materials, activity, and product options that include analytical and critical thinking skills.
- Accelerate vocabulary development through a variety of strategies and materials.
- Provide opportunities for "real world" investigations and experiences (For example, in-depth study on climate change, endangered animals, interviews with meteorologists, zoologists.

Accommodations to Access Learning
• Provide a stimulating educational environment where there are opportunities for critical and creative thinking. • Use advanced organizers for taking notes and outlines to help the students with sequencing information. • Provide adequate workspace with limited distractions. • Use computer/technology to research and complete projects. • Allow student choice to demonstrate learning. • Allow extra time to complete assignments/projects.

Explicit Instruction: Compensatory Strategies
• Instruct student in how to break new learning into manageable segments and use a timeline to plan steps needed to complete project. • Instruct student in the use of highlighters and color coding to note key information. • Teach research strategies and skills essential for in-depth study and advanced learning. • Use software programs. (For example, teach Inspiration software to aid students in organizing information, writing, and projects.) • Ask students to write down or log how long he thinks an assignment will take and record how long it actually took to complete. • Teach student how to avoid fatigue by taking frequent breaks.

Specific Instruction: Intervention/Remediation
• Teach typing and word processing. • Teach student how to organize reports and projects. • Teach student strategies for planning, revising, and editing written products. • Teach student how to prioritize assignments. • Teach student to use checklists to mark his progress.

Chapter 3
Getting it Right: Teachers, Schools, and Parents

A fundamental guiding principle for physicians is "First, do not harm." Doctors must consider the possible harmful effects that any intervention they recommend might have on their patients.

This principle also should guide those who work with children. Educational decisions made in schools every year should never be carried out until everyone who has a stake in them can say that the child's best interest was their primary concern, and that the child is likely to benefit without harm.

In my career with gifted students, I observed too many instances when the myths surrounding the "smart kid" permeated the decisions adults made, and the child suffered as a result. To get it right in school, we must eliminate the myths and deal with the reality of what gifted children need to reach their potential. Educators and parents must intervene early to advocate on behalf of the child who learns differently, particularly since these differences make learning and achievement difficult. All children have the right to a challenging and meaningful education. What do we mistakenly believe about gifted children? Here are some myths.

Myths and Truths

Myth: Gifted students are capable of teaching themselves and need little academic support.

Truth: There is a kernel of truth in this myth. If a gifted child grabs on to an area of interest, he may become an expert very quickly, sometimes even outstripping his teacher's knowledge. Most gifted students are adept at figuring out many things on their own. But not always; and if they have a learning disability, they may have difficulty applying this knowledge or conveying it to others, or they may miss some of the foundational information, which will handicap them later. If they don't understand something, particularly a basic concept, they may be reluctant to tell the teacher or parent for fear of being criticized or 'blowing their cover' as a 'smart kid'. Being unsure of fundamentals can trip them up as they move through the curriculum, and they may begin to doubt their own intelligence.

To fully develop their abilities, gifted students need guidance from well-trained teachers who challenge them and know how to differentiate lessons, so the students are engaged appropriately. Differentiation means tailoring lesson plans to better match student ability and therefore involve the student more because it is interesting to him. After the teacher has used assessment data to determine the student's needs, differentiation can take place with:

1. Content/input: the material presented
2. Process/sense-making: the activities used to practice or make sense out of the content
3. Product/output: Results of curricular activity which demonstrate student's learning and expansion of skills based on their own readiness, interest, and learning style.

Below are three examples of how teachers can differentiate lessons in content, process, and product for different content areas in school.

Table 3.1. Examples of How to Differentiate a Lesson

Content	Process	Product[56]
Subject: Reading **Topic**: Historical Fiction **Grades**: 5-8 **Skill**: Identify the characteristics of historical fiction. **Differentiation**: • Teachers provide a selection of historical fiction books that reflect a variety of reading levels and match the student with the appropriate historical fiction book.	**Subject:** Geography **Topic**: Coordinate Graphs **Grades 4-6** **Skill**: Plot data points and read coordinate graphs. **Differentiation:** • Tier 1: Create a brochure that shows how to plot points and read coordinate graphs. • Tier 2: Develop a game that has coordinates to move forward in the game. • Tier 3: After examining maps, students will make a map of their school and playground with different points of interest and their coordinates.	**Subject:** Spanish **Grades:** 9-12 **Skill:** Understand more fully how elements of a given culture interrelate and form a distinct personality of people. **Differentiation:** • Students will choose a mode of expression: write a travel guide, make a video/film documentary, present a drama, etc. • Students will investigate the history, religion, economics, education, climate, literature, art, language structure and how these elements are interrelated. • Students can choose to work alone or in a small group. • Advanced students will do cross-cultural comparisons.

We would never send talented athletes or musicians out onto the field or the stage without coaching them; we don't expect them to figure everything out by themselves. We show them how to perform by breaking a task down into fundamental skills and help them deliberately practice the skills repeatedly.[57] We investigate why certain things are easy for them, while other aspects are harder. We work with these athletes and musicians in practice, pointing out what they did right and what they need to improve. Why, then, would we expect a particularly able student to get academics on his own when we don't expect the same from a gifted football player or singer? Gifted students need sustained and careful coaching too.

Many studies about gifted children indicate they may be so far ahead of their same-age peers in certain areas that they know more than half of the grade-level curriculum before the school year begins.[58] In other areas, they may be at the level of average children their age, or even lag behind; or they may have knowledge and abilities but be unable to demonstrate it in the ways required in class. They are asynchronous in their abilities. The teacher needs to be aware of this situation because being gifted and uncomfortably ahead is as special a need as what is required by a child struggling to keep up. While most students may do fine with a standard curriculum, those at both ends of the curve require accommodation. In *Re-Forming Gifted Education*, Dr. Karen Rogers emphasizes that an individual education plan tailored to a child's needs is particularly important.[59] If we are willing to do it for the struggling student, we must be willing to do if for the child who is gifted.

Myth: Gifted students are either happy, popular, well-adjusted, and always excel in school, or they're nerds who will never fit in anywhere.

Truth: Many gifted children are indeed friendly, mature, self-aware, and emotionally adjusted. They get their work done, they're happy in school. A good educational fit can make a critical difference in the lives of gifted students. In her article, "*The Impact of Giftedness on Psychological Well-Being,*"[60] child psychologist Dr. Maureen Neihart postulates that if intellectually or academically gifted children participate in educational programs geared to their needs and receive support at home, they often will be well-adjusted and happy. However, if a smart child feels isolated, helpless and hopeless, it puts him at risk of developing more serious social and emotional issues.

Being gifted is no guarantee of success in school or life. While high intelligence can help make coursework—from kindergarten to college—easier to understand, it isn't the only determinant of how well a child will perform in school. Many other factors outside of intellect are important, too, such as self-concept, grit, mindset, organizational and study skills, supportive family, etc. Factors such as handling stress and social relationships also play a big part in a student's overall success.

Unfortunately, these non-intellectual factors cause problems for gifted people. They may become overly anxious, and their stress levels then impede their academic performance. For example, they may be a perfectionist: if they can't do it perfectly the first time, they may stop trying to master a skill or concept altogether.

Friendships can be difficult for children who are highly gifted. They often prefer the company of adults because other children may not understand what they're talking about. Such students can exhibit some degree of bossiness because they know how things *should* be done; their interests may be too esoteric for typical children to understand. They can be shut out by their own choice or by the actions of others. And when they find certain tasks to be difficult, they begin to doubt themselves because so many other areas are so easy for them that they discount their own personal worth, and their self-concepts suffer. As a result, they often feel isolated, and need strong social and emotional support from parents, teachers, and counselors.

Perhaps the most common social and emotional issue these children contend with is asynchronous development. This is a wide variation in abilities within the child, and also a mismatch between the children's chronological, physical, and intellectual ages. Such a child may at one moment be ready to discuss the Cretaceous Period in depth, and at the next moment be throwing a tantrum because his parents prohibit going to the library at dinner time.

The student may be a ten-year old in a five-year-old's body: highly advanced intellectually, but emotionally still a five-year old, unable to control his feelings. Usually, the more extreme the intellectual advancement, the more extreme the asynchrony.[61] It is very important for teachers and parents to assist asynchronous learners as they enter school and proceed in the early grades not only to understand themselves, but also to develop ways to help them manage their asynchrony. As they become older, the asynchrony is likely to level out in many areas, but some students feel burdened with it until they get to college.

Though some gifted children struggle, particularly those who are 2e, the majority of gifted students in general do not. They are often class leaders, athletes, active in music, drama, and school clubs, and involved in their communities.

Myth: Gifted students are good role models for other students, and they can provide challenge for the other students in the regular classroom.

Truth: Students who are not gifted do not usually look to their gifted classmates as role models. A struggling reader will not emulate a classmate who is reading several grade levels above his peers. In a Roeper Review article titled "*In Search of Reality: Unraveling the Myths about Tracking, Ability Grouping and the Gifted*," Ellen Fiedler, Richard Lang, and Susan Winebrenner[62] explain that students generally model their behavior on the behavior of others who are of similar ability and who are coping well in school. "If all the other students watch from the sidelines while the smart one provides the answers, their perceptions of themselves as competent, capable learners suffer."[63]

Being set up by teachers or parents as experts is not good for gifted learners either. If they discover they are being used as classroom role models or they are asked to teach other students, they may put intense pressure on themselves to be exceptional in every subject or may resent being used to teach others. Furthermore, most talented children are not gifted in every academic area. They may excel in math or language arts, but not in social studies or music. To force them to show the way for other students is unfair. They have the right to progress in their learning within their own sense of ability, and without undue burden.

Myth: In general, gifted students are pretty much alike.

Truth: No two students are alike, and like other children, each gifted child is unique. In fact, some experts have found that gifted children are more diverse than are children of average ability.[64] Although there are some characteristics that most gifted children share, like rapid learning, asking probing questions, and mature thinking, not all gifted students exhibit all the characteristics all the time. Teachers and parents should be aware of the broad categories of giftedness. These come from the federal definition of giftedness, defined in the 1972 Marland Report to Congress[65] and which is the basis for most state and local legislation.

- *General intellectual ability*, characterized by an advanced vocabulary and the ability to reason well, even with abstract problems.
- *Specific academic aptitude,* characterized by very high achievement in a particular academic discipline. They can easily exceed the standard curriculum and may need to be accelerated in that subject area.
- *Creative thinking and production,* characterized by exceptional ability in coming up with original ideas and by a lively, highly developed imagination.
- *Leadership/Psychosocial ability,* characterized by the ability to manage and organize other people and projects. They are highly responsible and can be relied upon to get the job done.
- *Psychomotor ability,* characterized by exceptional performance in such areas as sports because of their strength and agility and sense of themselves in space.
- *Ability in the visual and performing arts,* characterized by exceptional production in art, music, drama, or creative writing. They are original and imaginative in expressing their ideas.

By understanding the characteristics and behaviors specific to each category, caring adults can assist with the identification of gifted learners, including those who are 2e. Below are some of the specific behaviors for the categories of giftedness.

Table 3.2. Specific Behaviors for Categories of Giftedness

General Intellectual Ability	• Very good memory • Observant • Developmentally advanced in language and thought • May speak and read earlier than expected • May have large vocabulary for age • Grasp complex and abstract concepts/ relationships that normally are learned at an older age • Quick and logical thinker-asks lots of questions
Specific Academic Aptitude	• Long attention span in area of interest • Learns rapidly and easily and with less repetition in area of interest • Spends more time on subject of interest • Able to judge others in area of interest • In school, perform at the 95% at the national level on a standardized achievement test of specific academic ability in that field (math, language arts, science, social studies)
Creative Thinking and Production	• High energy • Sense of humor • Attracted to complexity • Open-minded • Intuitive • Can be emotional • Full of ideas • Constructs/builds, rebuilds • Irritated and bored by routine

Leadership and Psychosocial Ability	• Can get others to engage in tasks • Organize others based on their skills, personalities, and abilities • Communicate ideas, goals, and directions clearly • Understand how people feel and how groups function • Naturally exercise authority, reliably and responsibly • Looked to by others for ideas, suggestions, and decisions
Psychomotor Ability	• Coordinated, balanced and confident in physical activities • Full of energy • Shows endurance, stamina, and persistence in physical activities • Exhibits precision in motor skills • Challenged by difficult athletic activities • Good manipulative skills
Ability in Visual and Performing Arts	• Music: good sense of rhythm, unusual like for music and musical activities, responds to rhythm, melody, and harmony, makes up original tunes • Dramatics: uses voice to reflect changes in mood, effectively communicates feelings by means of facial expression, gestures, and bodily movements, enjoys evoking emotional responses from listeners • Art: loves drawing and does it well, shows originality in work, uses art to express feelings and experience, interested in other people's art and both appreciates it and critiques it • Literature: writes in journal/diaries/blogs, enjoys stories from books, television, etc. and then makes up own stories, vivid imagination and expresses it in words, evokes feelings from others with their own writing

Myth: Accelerated placement options are socially harmful for gifted students.

Truth: The research simply does not support this myth. In fact, it is to the contrary.[66] According to the National Association for Gifted Children, "educational acceleration is one of the cornerstones of exemplary gifted education practices."[67] Acceleration means matching the level, complexity, and pace of the curriculum with the readiness and motivation of the student. We should never ask a highly gifted six-year-old who reads and comprehends at a third-grade level to stay with his same-age peers for reading instruction. Acceleration options include single-subject acceleration, whole-grade-skipping, early entrance to school, dual enrollment (high school students taking college course for credit prior to graduation), International Baccalaureate and Advanced Placement (AP).[68]

In *A Nation Deceived: How Our Schools Hold Back American's Brightest Students*,[69] the authors argue for the academic acceleration of qualified gifted and talented students, based on the results of studies on outcomes of accelerating or not accelerating high-achieving students. The report presents the research on acceleration with the purpose of increasing the number of students who have access to the process.

In 2015, the follow-up report, *A Nation Empowered: Evidence Trumps the Excuses Holding Back American's Brightest Students*,[70] informed educators, parents, and policy makers about the most current research on acceleration, how that information has been applied to educational policy throughout the nation, and how educators can use the findings to make decision for their brightest students. If the results of the *Iowa Acceleration Scale* argue for acceleration, and teachers, parents, and the student agree with the assessment, and can work out such practical details as, for example, transportation to the middle school for an elementary school student, then acceleration can be a real lifesaver for the highly able student. As for twice-exceptional students, single subject acceleration with remedial tutoring and/or cluster grouping with other like students may be a good option.

Myth: Gifted students come from predominately white middle- and upper-class families.

Truth: Gifted and talented children are present in all cultural, ethnic, and socioeconomic groups, yet the various minorities are significantly under-identified as gifted and not placed in gifted classes. We are swayed by prejudicial cultural expectations for children from minority groups, so that educators overlook giftedness and related issues, and instead conclude simply that a child has a more obvious disability like ADHD or autism spectrum disorder. As Webb, et al (2018) have pointed out, "Many Black-American, Hispanic-American, or other minority cultural students end up in special education classes or are viewed as having behavior problems by their white teachers. Teachers don't nominate these students for gifted services. Parents from disenfranchised groups are less likely to know about resources for gifted children and adults, and they are often less able to afford outside testing and assessment or even know that options exist to get a second opinion. As a result, gifted programs in many schools are disproportionally white, and minority gifted children are more likely to have their intellectual abilities overlooked and their behaviors classified as disorders."[71]

Many of these students are denied the opportunity to maximize their potential because of the way in which programs and services are funded, and/or by flawed identification practices. Too many school systems still use only teacher surveys or checklists and other subjective performance indicators based on middle-class norms and values as part of their gifted and talented identification and programming process.

Test bias is also a very real concern when identifying gifted children from diverse populations because generally the tests administered in schools are still oriented to the language, culture, and experience of middle-class white students. Children from lower socioeconomic groups, children with limited English proficiency, and children with various hearing, speech, vision, or other learning impairments will rarely be referred for testing or identified if they are tested.

For some time, American gifted education proponents have been shining a light on the need for more appropriate procedures to identify culturally, linguistically, and ethnically diverse (CLED) students for advanced school programs. In *Increasing Diversity in Gifted Education*[72] the authors provide research-based strategies for identification and program services, so barriers are removed for talented students who are systematically underrepresented in programs and services for the gifted. Some of these strategies are listed here:

- Expand the definition of giftedness to ensure it is inclusive of unique characteristics of people from 'non-standard' non-White cultures.
- Use a variety of screening measures, not relying solely on intelligence assessments.
- Use local, as well as national, norms for standardized tools of assessment.
- Include student, parent, and educator interviews, work samples, portfolios, anecdotal information, rating scales, checklists, and surveys to help in identification.
- Look at the whole child, including cognitive, affective, and psychomotor/behavioral domains.
- Use culturally sensitive and non-verbal assessments, such as the Comprehensive Test of Non-Verbal Intelligence (CTONI), the Universal Non-Verbal Intelligence Test (UNIT), the Test of Non-Verbal Intelligence 4th Edition (TONI-4), or the Naglieri Nonverbal Ability Test (NNAT).
- Include creativity measures such as the Torrance Test of Creative Thinking.
- Provide professional development to teachers, counselors, and administrators on topics of immigration, poverty, and understanding other cultures, including language barriers.
- Translate into native languages the critical information the student/family must know about gifted referral and identification.

It is important to remember that ability and achievement scores should not be the only criteria for decision making in identifying students for gifted and enrichment programs. Research in gifted education has supported an expanded conception of giftedness. Therefore, in addition to aptitude and achievement, making decisions for special services should include course grades, portfolios of work, creativity, and teacher and parent ratings. As Joseph Renzulli, (a leader in gifted education) said, "When we change to a true multiple-criteria identification system, more services can be given to develop excellence in a greater number of students in an equitable and theoretically justified manner."[73] As for twice-exceptional children, it is imperative to use a multiple criteria identification system, or the student is very likely to be missed. Almost all 2e boys I have worked with would never have had the opportunity to participate in their schools' gifted and enrichment programs if only classroom teachers' assessments and grades were used to make the identification for referral.

Myth: All children are gifted.

Truth: All children have strengths and positive attributes, but not all children are intellectually gifted. Gifted and talented students have specialized needs when it comes to learning. This is even more the case when the child is 2e. They require particular modifications to the regular curriculum to ensure they are stimulated, challenged and learning new material, and they often must be taught with an approach completely different from the norm.

Many people feel uncomfortable with the term "gifted," believing it to be elitist and that it is unfair to give more to a child who already has so much. However, it is never elitist to allow a child the right to learn something new every day rather than relearn the same things again and again. People are not all alike, and to say that some children do not have greater intellectual ability or talent than others is simply false. We cannot hold children back just because we don't like the word "gifted." If gifted education is elitist, then so are varsity basketball teams, show choirs, and the National Honor Society, all of which require students to be selected from a larger group and given special experiences according to their readiness.

Myth: Gifted students work only for grades.

Truth: Gifted students usually like to make good grades, but they often refuse to work for grades alone, particularly if the work is repetitive. They are intellectually curious and are problem solvers who usually benefit from working on open-ended, interdisciplinary problems, particularly if those problems are relevant to their lives or to something they are interested in. In-depth projects that make an impact for the greater good, such as implementing an effective recycling program in their schools or creating an application for smartphones so disabled citizens can learn more about which restaurants and businesses are easily accessible in the community, are much more likely to motivate the gifted student than just getting another 'A'.

When smart children are not making the grades that parents and teachers expect, it is time to take a closer look at why. If the student is asked only to remember information and regurgitate it back for tests, it won't be long before he rebels. Grades could slip, and enthusiasm for school wane. Even the gifted child who thrives on all 'A's will begin to ask if there are opportunities to solve more challenging problems.

Schools should consider programs such as Destination Imagination (https://www.destinationimagination.org), a project-based learning program that blends science, technology, engineering, and mathematics principles with creative, collaborative problem-solving. Future Problem Solving (http://www.fpspi.org) is another program that stimulates critical and creative thinking skills, encourages students to develop a vision for the future and prepares them for leadership roles.

Myth: Gifted children learn the same way.

Truth: Some gifted children are "mappers" (sequential learners), while others are "leapers" (spatial learners.)[74] The mappers use a series of logical steps to respond to a given situation. They learn best by understanding details of a subject and slowly building an image of the bigger picture. This student can experience difficulties when he is impatient with the time-consuming details of reading or a math problem. Such students also get frustrated easily with people who don't understand things as quickly as they do.

The leapers think in pictures rather than words, and they learn holistically. They need to see the big picture and how the new material connects to information they have already learned. These students are often frustrated when they have a teacher(s) who instructs only with words. They must visualize in order to learn, and they do not benefit from rote or repetition.

Teachers and parents need to be keenly aware of how to help both types of learners. Here are some ideas:

Table 3.3. Types of Gifted Learners

Sequential "Mappers"	Holistic "Leapers"
Show an outline for the presentation of new material.	Give a short overview or summary of the topic then move to the details
Provide clear expectations with step-by-step directions.	Draw connections from specific details or information to the larger concepts.
Start with simpler concepts and build up to more complex ideas.	Allow student to work on problems or issues that encourage creative approaches.
Provide enough information to ensure success.	Allow student to skim or preview chapters and look ahead to advanced concepts.
Provide an example of what is expected.	Allow students to work at their own pace since they prefer the student-driven approach in their classrooms.
Include a time frame for completing assignments/projects.	Show visual images, diagrams, and graphs.
Include journals, learning logs, puzzles and logic games when planning lessons.	Relate learning to personal experiences, stories, and anecdotes.
Provide options to work at desks in orderly quiet surroundings.	Allow informal seating with music or other background noise.

Sequential "Mappers"	Holistic "Leapers"
Allow students to study alone and/or work on a single task without interruptions.	Provide opportunities for students to work in groups and/or work on several task simultaneously.

Myth: Gifted children always test well.

Truth: Gifted students make intellectual connections differently. They often think abstractly and with such complexity they may not be able to select one answer in a multiple-choice question because they can see how other answers might be correct. These students often need help with concrete study and test-taking skills. Such interventions can range from providing the child with time management plans for taking timed tests, to helping them understand quickly the intent of a question. Additionally, children are often asked to "show their work" to explain their thinking when it comes to solving a problem or issue, but this is difficult for both types of learners. The *leapers* may not know how they got a right answer, having simply intuited it, and the *mappers* may get lost in the steps leading to the right answer. Nonetheless, this requirement is often a part of standardized tests. While gifted students often do not require "grill and drill" standardized test preparation, they may need considerable help with the skill of 'showing work'.

Teachers also need to keep in mind that classroom differentiation does not apply only to how the content is delivered to their students. It also applies to how students are tested. One type of exam is not always appropriate for every student in a class. When a smart child consistently does poorly on certain types of tests, such as multiple-choice exams, the teacher may need to consider alternative test formats, such as oral exams, written assessments (activities in which the student selects or composes a response to a prompt), or performance tasks (hands-on-activities that require students to demonstrate their ability to perform certain actions). These alternatives are often effective in getting at what the student really knows, rather than what he can—or cannot—parrot back.

Some other simple factors can impede children's performance on tests. They include:

- *Child's maturity level*: Because of asynchronous development, a student may be ready for a test intellectually, but have difficulties with fine motor tasks, such as filling in bubbles or pressing the right key on a computerized test.
- *Poor testing skills*: A child may be unprepared for testing because he has not been given the tools to understand the test.
- *Test anxiety*: Gifted students sometimes freeze because they are worried that their answers may be wrong, resulting in less than a perfect score.
- *Attention problems*: Some students are daydreamers or easily distracted and may find that when the time is nearly up, they have to move quickly to finish the test. The results may be missed questions and nonsensical answers.
- *Motivation factors*: Some students, particularly smart children, may be totally unmotivated by *yet another test* that doesn't recognize their true abilities. They may become lackadaisical in answering, or even defiant, making their impatience with testing known because it doesn't describe them.
- *Environmental and personal test-taking factors*: Hunger, heat, noise, fatigue, or illness can lower scores.
- *Connections to the test administrator*: If the relationship with the test administrator is positive or negative based on previous interactions with the child, the test results can be affected.

Myth: Gifted children's emotions are like other children.

Truth: Sometimes this is true, but the more highly gifted the child, the more likely he is to demonstrate emotional intensity and particular sensitivity. Just as his thinking is more complex than other students, so are his emotions. Feeling everything more deeply than others can be both painful and frightening. Emotionally intense gifted children often have to cope with inner conflict, self-criticism, anxiety, and feelings of inferiority, very often brought on by a sense that they must do more than others, like write the perfect paper or solve one of the world's great problems.

The most important thing we can do to nurture emotionally intense gifted children is to accept them and their feelings. Though all children need to feel understood and supported, it is particularly important for gifted children, and they need to know it is normal for them to feel the way they do. In other words, we should help the child understand that experiencing emotions more intensely than others is part of their particular way of being. Parents and teachers can help them use their keen intellect and insight to develop self-awareness and self-acceptance.

Meeting Their Needs

Meeting the needs of these exceptional students can seem like a heavy burden. Classrooms are diverse today, with students from different cultural, religious, and socioeconomic backgrounds. Their interests and maturity levels vary as well. English may not be their first language. It may seem like too much work to provide strategies for students who are talented and achieving when other students need more of the teacher's time and help. This makes it even more challenging for a teacher to meet the needs of a 2e child.

In fact, because gifted children, whether 2e or not, may have an advanced knowledge of certain subjects or will comprehend new material with only one or two repetitions, they may become bored, disruptive, or both as they wait for their fellow students to catch up. Their insatiable curiosity and endless questioning may take teacher time away from students who are slower to grasp concepts and need more of the teacher's attention to come to proficiency. However, if gifted students are challenged appropriately and allowed to self-direct part of their learning, they are far less likely to either act out or turn off. The more teachers can engage their specific needs with independent work, the more time they will have to devote to students who need more assistance.

In addition to understanding these myths and truths about gifted children, schools should be more open to providing strategies that support the success of their students. Cluster grouping is one such strategy.

A Strategy that Works: Cluster Grouping

Cluster grouping refers to grouping roughly three to six identified children with a teacher trained in the education of gifted students for at least part of the day. Some people believe that cluster grouping is a form of "tracking" students. This is incorrect. Tracking organizes entire classrooms by ability, and students tend to remain in these groups for the remainder of their school experience.

In cluster grouping, children of similar readiness in an area of study are grouped, but they may be regrouped with a different set of students to learn a different subject. This provides opportunities for gifted children to learn new material every day, and it encourages them to excel because they are learning alongside students who are at a similar level of proficiency and readiness in that area. They don't get egotistical about how much smarter they are because the students with whom they are learning are equally proficient. They feel at home, not different or alone. They find it easier to make friends with others in the cluster group. This can be particularly important for kids who are 2e since their skills and abilities are likely to range over a broader area. They may be gifted in their cluster group for math, but far less able in a language arts group.

Another important reason to group smart students together is that gifted services can be directly applied to the classrooms with these children, which makes it highly efficient and cost-effective. Too many times I have experienced serving multiple classes at one grade level because the children I worked with were placed in many different classrooms: one with Miss Johnson, two with Mr. Rodriquez, and four with Mrs. Montoya, and so on, until all the gifted children were distributed within that grade. Spreading the children around like this makes it harder for the teachers and/or gifted interventionist to work productively, while cluster grouping with a single teacher represents a mindful way to make sure gifted students continue to receive the most appropriate instruction. "This method of managing instruction for gifted and talented children makes good sense in practical terms."[75]

Cluster grouping helps both gifted and 2e students stay focused. Because academics come easily to many gifted children, they may believe they will never have to struggle to learn. As for twice-exceptional learners, they are more likely to focus on what does not come easily to them and they become frustrated. Both groups of gifted students may not develop study habits or may become lazy and disengaged from learning in school. The most effective way to keep them excited about learning is to place them in cluster groups with other gifted children who are like them and to assign them rigorous, relevant work that challenges them appropriately and provides them with some measure of control over their own learning.

One smart boy I worked with in elementary school avoided taking any advanced placement classes when he got to high school. He knew these classes would prepare him for the collegiate learning environment he desired, but he chose to register for the basic level coursework because he lacked the study and organizational skills necessary for attempting more difficult courses. (Most of the 2e students I work with have problems with study and organizational skills, which impedes their success in school.) Although this boy certainly could have excelled in advanced placement classes, he was afraid to try. Because the early school experiences were too easy for him, he never had a reason to develop the abilities he needed when he was offered a more challenging environment in high school.

It benefits everyone when schools match the program to the child and support appropriate grouping needs for their smart students.

How Can Parents Get It Right? Parenting Styles

Tailoring curricula for students is just as important as it is for parents to examine their parenting styles and determine if they are helping or hindering their child's success in school.

Gifted children are happiest when their parents accept their uniqueness and support their interests. The parents must be the trusted allies in a world that may not understand the child. However, parents also must impose limits and discipline while allowing the child a degree of autonomy that matches the student's level of maturity. Certain parenting styles do not work well with most children, and for gifted students they can be a disaster.

Bold.

One student with whom I worked could never seem to find the button that made his mother happy. He thought if he made all A's on his report cards, he would ease the tension at home. But there was always something for the child to improve upon in his mother's eyes. The school environment was never satisfactory either, so this child developed emotional problems and had trouble managing social situations.

Authoritarian.

I clearly remember a student with a domineering father. The child's decisions, when he made them, were based on his father's desires. For example, this student was not athletic and did not enjoy sports. However, because the father constantly pressured his son to play a sport (since he himself excelled at them), the son joined a baseball league. The experience brought the child great unhappiness, but he continued to follow his father's wishes. As the student got older, he resisted opportunities to choose for himself so as to avoid antagonizing his father.

My partner in gifted education at the middle school later told me that this same student was very creative and wanted to perform in the school play. However, he did not try out because his father said that participating in drama was not important to his son's future. I heard later that when this student got to the high school, he became so resistant towards authority figures that staff did not know if he would make it to graduation. (A moving portrayal of this parent/student dynamic at work can be found in the Academy Award nominated film *Dead Poets Society*.)

Permissive.

One student's mother was very loving but had few guidelines and rules. She wanted to avoid confrontations with her son. If he broke one of the few rules his mother made, he was rarely disciplined. It seemed she was more interested in being her son's best friend. Because she was so awed by her son's obvious intelligence, he was allowed to make important family decisions as he got older. By middle school, he felt more like his mother's peer than her son. The lack of discipline in this student's home caused the student's attitude towards other adult authority figures to be tarnished, and clashes with teachers became common.

Overambitious.

Because a gifted child may have boundless energy, parents may overschedule him and then expect exceptional performance across a variety of activities. I remember two parents who filled every moment of their son's days and weekends with structured activities at which he was expected to excel.

On Mondays, when I asked my students about their weekends, this young boy explained his schedule in detail. The student was an exceptional age-group swimmer who spent untold hours in the pool. He often traveled to meets many miles away from home. Sometimes these events took place over holidays. Team sports were also infused into his schedule depending on the seasons. When I asked this student what he did for fun on the weekends, he did not know how to respond. I often wished I had heard him say he went to the movies with friends and had a great time.

By the time Monday morning rolled around, he was exhausted. He had had no time to recharge his battery for the new school week. It would have been a much different story if my student had described his weekend activities with joy. But each Monday morning he simply said, "I'm tired."

Although a gifted child with excessive energy may thrive and do well in a plethora of activities, never seeming to tire, this boy would have benefited from more downtime. I was happy to hear that when he was in seventh grade, swimming, which he loved, was the only scheduled activity he continued. He dropped all other sports in favor of a couple of school clubs and some relaxation and fun.

Uninvolved

Many years ago, I knew a very smart boy who was raised by a single mother. Two of his brothers were always in trouble at school and later with the law. The mother was too often overwhelmed by their issues, and the student was on his own most of the time. In middle school, this smart boy received many accolades for his achievements, but when school banquets were held for students to receive their awards, his mother was never present. Over time, I watched this student become emotionally withdrawn. He was stressed and anxious because he was basically raising himself without help or guidance.

There is no question that gifted children can be a handful, and there are times when parents feel alone and defeated when trying to figure out the right balance of love, discipline, challenge, sympathy, toughness, rules, and freedom. With support and help from other parents and professionals, many of the problems can be alleviated.

Because 2e children are all different, it is difficult to know which parenting style works best for each one. Nonetheless, all parents should empower a twice-exceptional student to overcome their disability. They should never rush to rescue them when they appear to struggle, nor should they make them feel that they are not good enough. By helping the child to meet their challenges with their own skills and ambition, parents enable their child to build self-esteem. This can be a great victory for a child who often doesn't feel they match up to adult ideals. Below are some strategies to promote positive social and emotional development in the 2e child.

Table 3.4. Strategies to Promote Social and Emotional Development of Twice-Exceptional Children[76]

Strategy	Description
Create a safe home environment.	Reassure the child they are loved and appreciated, allow the child to vent their frustrations at home that may have built up at school, make sure the child contributes at home with ideas and plans and the contributions are valued.

Strategy	Description
Nurture strengths and interests.	Encourage the child to explore their strengths and interests so they become motivated to learn; this builds confidence that they can succeed in the face of challenges.
Foster "I can do it" attitude.	Help the child learn that all tasks require effort and persistence to complete; praise the child's effort not ability; encourage the child to use positive self-talk.
Support the development of compensatory strategies.	Encourage the use of graphic organizers (homework and projects), technology (increase productivity), spelling and grammar checkups (for editing papers), and calendar tools like Microsoft Outlook (organize time and projects)
Promote positive coping strategies	Discourage avoidance, distancing from a problem, and learned helplessness; promote and encourage accepting responsibility for one's actions, dealing with unrealistic expectations, seeking proper help, and becoming a self-advocate.
Coach realistic goal setting.	Begin with short-term goals that result in success. Increased success leads to motivation to strive for long term goals when they are broken into several achievable short-term goals. Celebrate successes.

Working for the Child

Parents of gifted children have another important role to fill: Advocate. To advocate means to champion, encourage, and uphold the child. It does not mean to attack, demean, or blame school officials or others. Parents who work cooperatively with teachers and schools have much greater success than those who go to war with them. This is particularly important for parents of twice-exceptional children to understand. Because frequent contacts will be necessary between home and school to support the special needs of the child and help him reach his potential, parents should remember:[77]

1. Approach problems as an opportunity to learn.
2. After all the facts are collected about a problem, approach the school/teacher with care and sensitivity to schedule a meeting.
3. Start a conference with positive comments and then communicate clearly and without blame. Keep the focus on the child's needs.
4. Always express a willingness to help resolve the problem and work collaboratively toward a positive solution.
5. Keep the lines of communication open for all follow-up meetings that will occur.

Because parents cannot always assume that the school staff will initiate a change in the school curriculum for a special student, they must concentrate on asking the right questions. Before this can occur, it is important for parents to do the following. First, learn about 2e children. Second, learn about gifted educational strategies and options. Third, find out what is offered at school to support their child's needs. Then, the parent will be better prepared to ask questions like: 1) Would my child benefit from being assigned to a specific teacher who understands twice-exceptionality? 2) Could the curriculum be compacted so my child can move more quickly through the material in the area of his strength? 3) Should my child be accelerated in a particular subject, or should he skip an entire grade level?

Parents want to find the best educational fit for their smart child so he can stay engaged, motivated, and feel accepted in school, but sometimes they don't know how to go about it. They might say, "If I ask for special accommodations for my child, I might rock the boat for him." Or "I don't want any special treatment for my child. I want him to feel like everyone else at this school." It is not 'rocking the boat'; and everyone does NOT feel the same! The point I try to make when I hear such statements is that their child *is* different, and his special needs must be addressed to see continued growth *and* avoid possible harm in school and at home.

Fear of reprisal by school staff should not be the family's focus. This happens so rarely that it really should be thought of as a myth unless parents approach the school in a 'full attack' mode and go straight to the principal, superintendent, or school board. By contrast, when parents come forward to discuss their child's educational needs with the school, they are sending a message that they understand their child, are concerned for his well-being, and they would like to be part of a team to make positive change for him.

To begin the process, parents need to determine what their child's strengths are and decide what goals they would like to accomplish in his school. It is essential for the twice-exceptional child's strengths to be identified and properly addressed so the student realizes success is possible in school. Also, if giftedness goes unnoticed while attending only to a student's leaning deficits, the student will not reach his potential, will become unhappy in school, and will possibly be at risk for leaving school all together.

One parent I worked with determined her 2e son's strength by observing several things. First, her son's achievement test results were consistently far above grade level in language arts. She noticed he also excelled in reading and writing in his regular classroom. Then she heard her son say that he was not feeling challenged anymore in his regular language arts class; he lost interest.

She spoke with me and others about the possibility of subject acceleration for her son in language arts. As part of the school's intervention assistance team, I collected more information, and it became clear that my student was an excellent candidate for single-subject acceleration. If the parent had not been alerted to her son's strength in language arts and the need for him to move more quickly through the curriculum, this child would most likely be sitting in his grade-level language arts class with very little new learning taking place. Today, however, he is the author of a popular self-published children's book.

Another route parents can take to make sure their child's educational needs are being addressed is to meet with the parents of other gifted children. Although no two children are alike, families of gifted children share similar characteristics and can find support and suggestions from each other to help make school and home life better. Supporting Emotional Needs of the Gifted (https://www.sengifted.org) is a nonprofit organization (founded by the late Dr. James T. Webb) that empowers families and communities to guide gifted and talented individuals to reach their goals. Help is available online, including parenting groups, webinars by top experts in the gifted field, and compelling articles on topics like misdiagnosis. It helps to be able to talk with other parents about what they have tried with their children and with the schools, particularly if a child is 2e.

Parents can also begin to advocate as a group. For example, one small parent group prepared a presentation for their school board that resulted in the district's creating a different language arts curriculum for the gifted children at the middle school level. The National Association for Gifted Children (www.nagc.org) has affiliated groups in every state that offer programming, advocacy, support, and annual state conferences.

Parents are the single most important influence in a child's development, outlook, and fulfillment of talent.[78] They must be the child's primary advocates. Advocacy works, and positive change for gifted children is attainable.

As we think about smart children in our homes, schools, and society, we must continually ask ourselves if we are doing everything possible to help these children reach their full potential as scholars and human beings.

The 2e boys you will read about in the next few chapters (whose identities have been changed), are very different high-potential students, yet they share similar problems in school. I worked with them in their gifted programs and advocated for positive change in ways that made their educational experience more enjoyable and productive.

Through the many activities, projects, and discussions we shared in my classes, it struck me that these 2e boys had one thing in common. They began school very excited to learn new things and to be valued unconditionally. However, they felt that the focus was almost always on their problems, and they were often made to feel that their giftedness was somehow a flaw their teachers wanted to alter. Fortunately, during these times, important people stepped forward to ease the struggles they experienced. Parents, teachers, and specialists helped put important plans into place to straighten the crooked paths they traveled through school.

As you read about Mateo, Jamal, Melvin, and Jake, remember they represent the many twice-exceptional boys in our schools who enter the doors of their classrooms looking for engagement with peers, teachers, and the curriculum. However, after a short time, they often find themselves locked in a struggle trying to get their specific needs met. They need regular educational structure to accommodate their overall program and their social and emotional needs in general; but they also need a curriculum customized for their gifts and challenges, including trained interventionists and appropriate acceleration. (Note: Many gifted children need regular instruction in one or more grade level subjects, but they may also need accommodations for an area of strength. A trained gifted specialist can help provide for this need.)

If your child or student looks like one of these, begin early to examine the ways in which you can nurture his excitement for learning before he "turns off" and loses that positive motivation. Help him understand his strengths as well as his challenges.

Part II:
Four Gifted Boys: Mateo, Jamal, Melvin, and Jake

Chapter 4
Mateo's Story: Gifted with Marked Asynchronous Development and ADHD

Getting to Know My Student

Because Mateo was the oldest child in his family, he had no preconceived ideas about school. All he knew was he could not wait to start kindergarten. Mateo was friendly, and he enjoyed playing with other children. On many occasions he told older friends, "I wish you could come over to my house and play games with me!"

However, by second grade, the excitement Mateo once had about school had died. His classroom environment was not welcoming to any child who "seemed" different, and Mateo was different. He was the child in the class who walked to the beat of his own drum. Although Mateo wanted to keep learning and playing with his classmates, like he had done in kindergarten and first grade, he began to fear his teacher. His ADHD behaviors disrupted her otherwise well-organized classroom and lesson plans, and Mateo received repeated criticism. His personality began to change as result.

The school did, however, recognize that Mateo had unusual abilities in several areas, and he was eligible for some gifted programming. One day while he attended my class for gifted children, he asked, "Why is your classroom different?" His keen observations of the world were telling him something was not right in school. He felt forced to behave one way in his regular classroom (subdued and quiet), yet when he felt comfortable and accepted by a teacher, such as in the gifted class, he felt comfortable being himself, smart and funny.

By third and fourth grade, things got better for Mateo; he found more stability in school because his teachers were more understanding of his special needs. He also seemed to get back to his old self when he was given opportunities to share his interests with others. For example, Mateo was delighted the day he brought his pet snake, Sammy, to school and explained how he cared for it. He said to his parents, "I am so happy! My teacher and friends seem to like my snake as much as I do."

Parenting Mateo

> *"His mind is always running. It would be nice to turn if off for a while."*
>
> -Mateo's father

Mateo's parents say their son developed normally as an infant. He walked at around the age of one, and he didn't talk much until he was about two years old. However, Mateo would get so frustrated about not being able to communicate and get what he wanted that he would bang his head on floors, walls, and tables. Mateo was unusually observant about his surroundings and would remember things his parents hardly noticed. He enjoyed stacking and sorting items. All these things might have suggested autism, but Mateo's parents began to think that his frustration might stem more from his intense curiosity.

Around two, Mateo demonstrated being a master puzzle solver. He loved completing puzzles for children around ages 4-6. His mother noticed he had a very specialized way of putting them together as well. If he worked on a puzzle such as Thomas the Tank Engine, he would separate the characters from the buildings. Then he would start with the most difficult pieces first. He would never start with the edge pieces the way many people do because he thought that was too easy. In addition to putting together advanced puzzles, Mateo was also great at memory games. His parents recall that when their son was four years old, they were astounded by how well he remembered the location of memory cards. Mateo's dad said, "He would beat us even when we were trying."

When Mateo entered kindergarten, his parents described him as a child who had a hard time controlling himself. He was a free spirit who looked at things from a completely different viewpoint than most. His personality was both goofy and introspective, and not everyone appreciated those personality traits. When he was in school, he had difficulty fitting into the frame some teachers created. However, if a teacher tried to understand his need for alternative ways of completing assignments and provided flexible learning options, Mateo did very well. At home, his parents struggled with whether to allow him the freedom he desired as he explored his environment, or to limit his behaviors to help him gain a better footing in school. (They considered setting firm time limits for completing household activities and homework so he understood that schoolwork should be completed on time. Also, they questioned whether they should discourage free exploration around their neighborhood because children are seldom allowed freedom to roam freely in their schools.)

Once Mateo was identified gifted in first grade, his parents thought, "great, he's really smart; he will get good grades and excel in life." However, they underestimated the problems their son would have as he progressed in school. When Mateo entered second grade and issues like not finishing classwork, failure to follow directions, and their son's overall unhappiness, escalated, it was eye-opening for his parents to hear from me, the school's gifted specialist, that their son had special needs and would never be a typical student.

Managing Mateo's high demand to learn new material, while at the same time addressing his inability to focus, complete work assignments, and correct inappropriate behaviors, was going to be a difficult balancing act for the parents of this smart boy. Mateo's dad said, "I was advanced at a young age and dealt with a lot of the same issues my son deals with, so I thought he might struggle a little with behaviors and focus issues. But I underestimated them."

Mateo's parents learned quickly that developing a close relationship with their son's teachers was essential. Helping him required frequent communication about Mateo's educational needs, a free exchange of information about 2e boys, and patience when teachers and parents did not see eye to eye about how best to support Mateo.

Mateo's parents once told me, "We don't know what's expected of the parents of children in special education classes, but we are quite sure there is little sympathy for parents whose kids are gifted." More than once they received negative responses when they told people their son was in a gifted program. In addition, when they elaborated that Mateo had some difficulties in school because of his giftedness, they felt as though some folks tried to bring them down a peg as parents of a smart child. This was baffling to them. However, these reactions to conversations with others who did not fully understand children's giftedness fueled their desire to learn more about their son's special needs and to serve as his advocate, as well as to advocate for other children like Mateo.

In addition to not receiving a lot of sympathy from adults regarding their son's school issues, Mateo's parents learned that schools approached children of different abilities in a variety of ways. In their case, they felt they had to "force" their son's school to meet his special needs so he could continue to reach his potential. At times, the reactions they experienced from some school staff were so stressful they felt there would be no choice but to move Mateo to a different school.

For example, one of Mateo's teachers, in apparent frustration, repeatedly emailed his parents and asked, "How should I work with your son? He is not responding to the in-class discipline system." Clearly, she did not know how to adapt her discipline system to accommodate special needs children like Mateo. That experience (and others) made Mateo's parents think the expectations for gifted children and special education children were not the same.

It seemed to them that the teachers bent over backwards to support their special education students with multiple interventions and an abundance of patience. But when it came to Mateo, they threw their hands up in frustration after knowing him only a short time. Mateo's father was certain the parents of special education students never got phone calls from their child's school expressing frustration about their child's lack of progress. In their view, the support these two different groups of children received in school was like night and day.

As Mateo traveled through elementary school and continued to experience a bumpy ride that affected his education, his parents asked themselves such questions as:

- ❍ Is Mateo just immature compared to his peers?
- ❍ Did we make a mistake entering our son in kindergarten instead of waiting a year?
- ❍ Did we choose the right school for our son to attend?
- ❍ Are we too easy on him at home?

Regardless of how they answered these questions, they believed Mateo would succeed in school if he had the right teacher guiding him. His mother explained that the most influential teachers never made Mateo feel as if there was something wrong with him. By contrast, Mateo experienced a few teachers who wanted to "repair" him because he didn't match their rigid expectations. These were generally very unproductive years in his education because Mateo felt that if he was failing in his teacher's eyes, he shouldn't even bother to try.

However, he responded well to teachers who were kind and appreciated his sense of humor. They weren't pushovers when he got silly, but they gently guided him back on course and challenged him with appropriate work. Overall, teachers who did not strive for perfection, but instead encouraged their students to reach appropriate goals, were the ones Mateo went out of his way to please.

Mateo's parents always knew their son had great intelligence, but when he had the opportunity to attend gifted education classes, they saw him "explore, expand, and untie his mind" in ways he never could in his regular classrooms. In reading the quarterly newsletters I wrote for parents to update them on the various activities and projects completed in my classes, Mateo's parents were pleased to see that their son had the opportunity to try creative and critical thinking activities at an advanced level. It was evident to them that their son was receiving individualized attention and working on content tailored to his strengths. They often said, "If it were up to us, Mateo would be in the gifted program all day and every day." Finally, Mateo found friends in his gifted class and was able to share playdates and activities like other children-and those experiences were invaluable to him.

Attention Deficit Hyperactivity Disorder

Regardless of the interventions made for him, as elementary school progressed, Mateo still exhibited behaviors such as lack of focus, fidgetiness, and unfinished tasks, and his mother was concerned he might have attention deficit disorder. She met with his pediatrician who requested both parent and teachers complete the rating scales from the Behavior Assessment System for Children (BASC). This instrument includes a set of measures for the assessment and identification of school-age children with emotional disturbances and behavioral disorders. It also provides a multidimensional understanding of the child and assists in the design of treatment plans with evidence-based interventions.[79] The doctor also wanted to speak with Mateo to gather additional information on possible co-existing conditions like language problems, anxiety, or depression. Because the pediatrician's analysis seemed thorough, Mateo's parents decided against further testing by a neuropsychologist. Mateo's mother's instincts were confirmed. Her son had ADHD. This diagnosis finally explained why Mateo was having difficulty achieving in school.

Note: As stated in: *Misdiagnosis and Dual Diagnoses of Gifted Children and Adults* (Webb et al., 2016), "Diagnosing ADHD warrants a thoughtful, complete evaluation, which includes awareness of the person's cognitive and emotional abilities along with the family, educational, and occupational context."[80]

The pressing question became whether to treat Mateo's ADHD with medication. His parents never had been proponents of giving medications to their children other than for illness. They now understood, however, that they had a twice-exceptional child who required special help, and medication was something they now had to consider.

As school continued, Mateo completed only one-third of his classwork and his change in behavior prompted his teacher to arrange a conference. She explained that Mateo seemed tired by mid-morning and didn't finish anything he started. Finally, when his mother heard the teacher mention that he required constant redirection when instructions were given, she and her husband knew they had to make a choice about medication.

They were uneasy about that decision. They were concerned about the potential side effects and worried that medication might change his personality or inhibit his ability to develop his own coping mechanisms. However, after the parent/teacher conference, they realized Mateo was heading down a difficult road.

By November of Mateo's third grade year, things were not better. He was very impulsive, and things were going downhill. Mateo's parents decided that no matter how many accommodations were offered in class, they would not be enough to provide the focus he needed to be successful in school, and so he began taking medication. His mother explained it would help him focus on learning, much like children who wear glasses to see better. Mateo accepted this analogy, but told his parents, "I don't feel smart anymore." This comment helped them understand that his self-esteem was eroding, and they moved forward, hoping the medication would help him feel better about himself.

It wasn't long before Mateo began to show a can-do spirit about his life, and he was motivated to do the right things at home and school. The small, attainable goals that had been set for him were met and rewarded. The progress Mateo was making also enabled him to rebuild his self-esteem. His parents had underestimated how much their son had struggled before, and when they saw the positive changes at home as well as at school, they realized they had made the right decision to use medication to treat Mateo's ADHD.

It is important to note that though Mateo was correctly diagnosed with ADHD, this diagnosis often is attached to students who simply have abundant energy and difficulty sitting still. These are often traits found in gifted children-and not every gifted jumpy kid has ADHD. It is a medical diagnosis and not one that should be made by a classroom teacher or administrator. In addition, although medication worked for Mateo, the medication decision must be carefully thought out and may not be appropriate for every situation.

Teaching Mateo

The gifted identification process across the United States varies widely. Some states, such as California, Michigan, and Wyoming, do not mandate identification. It is for this reason that we may never know how many gifted children are in our schools. We may miss over half of them. Some states require screening, but it is often left up to a school district to determine when and how this will be done-and what will be done with the results. It seems ludicrous that some states have a mandate to test, but not to serve, these exceptional students.

Some schools test whole groups by grade levels and others test only those children who are nominated by their teachers or parents. Fortunately for Mateo, his school screened all students beginning in first grade. If this had not occurred, he might never have been identified as gifted. His substandard performance on many early skills led some to believe he had a learning disability. This observation alone would have led teachers to focus solely on trying to remediate his challenges, and he might never have been provided the opportunities to focus on and develop his strengths, which were extraordinary.

Mateo's parents had done a good job observing their son's strengths and areas of need as he approached pre-school age. But it wasn't until he started a full-day school schedule that his teachers noticed discrepancies in his behaviors and learning that altered the path he traveled in school.

Kindergarten

Mateo was one of the youngest children in his kindergarten class. Mateo's preschool teacher was the first person to use the word "gifted" to describe him, although he was not identified as such. She told his parents he demonstrated the ability to think about things in interesting ways. Also, his pre-kindergarten screening indicated Mateo was well above average in ability. Despite his advanced abilities, many family members and friends advised his parents to hold him back from entering school for another year because of his youth.

The tipping point, though, for Mateo's parents to register their son for kindergarten this year instead of waiting was based on two things. First, they saw Mateo's frustration when he came home from his half-day preschool class. Mateo seemed to want to stay at school all day. Second, many anecdotal stories with others, including school staff, indicated Mateo's thinking ability was advanced for his age.

However, shortly after beginning his first year of *full day* schooling, Mateo's parents received an email from his teacher describing a child who had trouble responding to the way she disciplined students. In the color-coded behavior card system used by the teacher, Mateo almost always was on orange, the color that represented a student's constantly needing redirection. Because Mateo had enjoyed the half-day preschool program he attended and seemed to be excited by the idea of kindergarten, his parents were puzzled and immediately wondered if their decision to enroll their son in full-day kindergarten was a mistake. Mateo now dreaded going to school.

Unfortunately, Mateo's kindergarten teacher had overlooked both the information collected by his preschool teacher and his kindergarten screening results. She saw Mateo only as a discipline problem.

First Grade

First grade began poorly, Mateo had trouble with basic social cues like facial expressions and personal space. In addition, he had difficulty following directions, completing assignments, and writing. Despite the individualized attention his teacher gave to students who struggled, she had real concerns about Mateo. She felt that although he was clearly bright, he acted more like a kindergartener. His communication and sense of humor were advanced. He looked at things in a much different way from his peers such as questioning rules, asking "quirky" unexpected questions, and expressing a broader knowledge about some topics than his peers. Because Mateo felt his teacher was kind to him, he wanted to please her. He tried his very best on everything she instructed him to do in class, but he just could not meet first-grade standards and expectations. These included first grade academic skills in math, reading, and language arts, and social and emotional skills like gaining more independence, understanding right from wrong and forming friendships.

In the first grade, students took the CogAT, a cognitive ability test that measures verbal, quantitative, and nonverbal general reasoning abilities, and compares the results with children's age mates in the same grade level. Mateo's teacher was concerned he would not be able to give his best effort on this test because it would take several periods over a few days to complete, and she had a gut instinct that he was a very smart kid who had some maturity issues. In spite of her intuition, however, even she was surprised at the test results. Mateo's composite score was 140. This put him in the high range of ability; Mateo was identified gifted.

Asynchronous Development

With this important identification came the discussion of asynchronous development. Since kindergarten, Mateo's social and emotional development had lagged behind his intellectual abilities. He was often unable or unwilling to conform to the school's expectations because his development was out of whack.

Asynchronous development, where judgement and self-control trail behind intellect, is often a telltale sign of giftedness, especially in young children. However, "Many children, as they grow older, find that the abilities that once lagged behind do catch up."[81] Asynchronous development is also frequent in gifted children across their various intellectual abilities, where some areas are quite advanced, but others lag behind. Mateo had a strong sense of the concepts being taught, but he was unable to complete basic developmental tasks like writing his name and reading basic sight words. The main concern for a child like this is that he not be damaged socially and emotionally in the first few years of school. To prevent this from happening, the student needs to spend a large part of his day in a supportive environment with adults who understand that one size does not fit all when it comes to educating a child-like Mateo, and who can still provide the varied academic experiences that are needed.

When I met with Mateo's parents after the first-grade testing, they were mystified. Their child had been identified as a discipline problem in kindergarten, and he struggled to keep up in first grade. Now they were being told their son was identified gifted. How could that be? They wanted to know how they could help Mateo. They were not sure if they should focus on the developmental delays or learn more about the gifted label he had now been given.

I told them that asynchronous development was common in super-smart children. The most important thing was not to put additional stress on Mateo at his young age by telling him he had to work harder or that he was not doing his best. To do this would only cause the situation in first grade to go terribly off course and possibly result in irreparable harm as he grew up.

After I worked with Mateo in my gifted classes, I helped his parents and teacher by providing some books and websites (some included information about 2e) for them to learn more about raising and teaching a gifted child. I outlined educational approaches used in my classroom that were particularly helpful for Mateo to succeed: allowing choice of activities based on student interest; teaching critical and creative thinking skills like mind-mapping, visualization, and questioning; and modifying assignments with technology like typing or recording essays. I told them that even though gifted programs in schools are essential for children like Mateo, it is just as important for the child's academic, social, and emotional needs be met daily at home as well as in the regular classroom. Otherwise, the student feels the only place he can be understood and challenged is in the gifted classes.

I helped the teacher realize that some of the characteristics Mateo exhibited in class, like solving advanced number puzzles, asking probing questions, and interest in doing things differently, were tied to his giftedness. Once she understood that, she began to integrate accommodations that would support him in the classroom. Some examples the teacher began to try included: allowing more movement in the classroom, utilizing more visuals when she taught lessons, reducing the length and number of assignments, and providing checklists for tasks that were due by the end of the day. With both parents and teachers working together, it was possible to make sound educational choices as Mateo moved forward in school.

The Importance of the Teacher

One of the biggest decisions schools can make for children with special needs is the choice of the classroom teacher they will work with for an entire school year. As Mateo was finishing first grade, I spoke with the principal about possible placements for him in second grade. He needed a teacher who was nurturing and could accept his differences, but who also could be flexible and try new approaches to support his areas of strength as well as his areas of need. His first-grade teacher had done a very good job helping Mateo make progress in all areas of development, and his second-grade teacher needed to do the same.

During the conversation, the principal told me that one of the two second-grade teachers was retiring. Therefore, decisions about class placement for the new school year would have to wait until the new teacher had been hired. I mentioned that Mateo would not fit well with the remaining teacher because she taught to the whole class rather than individualizing her instruction, ran her class in a very structured way like a well-oiled machine, and allowed no room for errors. This would not be a helpful environment for Mateo. I was hopeful the principal would consider our discussions before placing Mateo in his new classroom. If he ran off the road by being placed with the wrong teacher, it would have devastating results.

Second Grade

Before second grade began, I received an email from Mateo's parents letting me know they had read several books and articles about parenting 2e children. They now understood their son had special needs and required support at home and at school.

At the top of the list of things they grasped from their reading was that they should stop punishing their son at home for behaviors that were out of his control. In addition, Mateo's family would learn to appreciate their son's sense of humor and silliness, and not shut him down like so many other adults in his life had tried to do. This turning point in the family's thinking had a very positive impact on Mateo.

As the new school year began, I discovered that Mateo and the other gifted children in second grade had been placed with the teacher about whom I had grave concerns, because she gave individual student attention a back seat to class conformity. The principal felt that this teacher with 'greater experience' would be a better fit for the gifted students. Sadly, it turned out to be the worst fit possible for Mateo.

In the very first quarter of second grade, he experienced tremendous stress. His teacher and parents weren't happy either. One of the first comments from Mateo's teacher was, "I cannot understand why a smart boy behaves the way he does in my class." There were no encouraging or positive comments on the papers he brought home. His parents assumed the worst about their son's performance in second grade, and they often punished him when he brought home a paper not up to his teacher's standards (even though they had promised themselves they wouldn't.) It was not surprising, therefore, when Mateo came home one day and said he hated school.

The tension during the first parent-teacher conference was palpable. The teacher shared her frustration that Mateo was not meeting grade-level benchmarks and the parents shared how they knew their son was capable of much better work than the samples that came home. Towards the end of the meeting, Mateo's parents decided it was important for them to hear about positive strides Mateo was making, rather than constant harsh criticism. They pointed out to his teacher that their son's self-esteem was beginning to suffer from the many negative comments on his work. When the meeting ended, the parents were assured they would receive more detailed communication about Mateo's progress, which could help with adjusting expectations and goals at home.

By the winter break things in Mateo's classroom had gone from bad to worse. His parents had not seen one paper with positive comments. In fact, they were seeing more and more critical notes. They had not received the promised emails and correspondence regarding Mateo's progress.

Mateo's dislike for school and his parents' frustration levels were at an all-time high. Another conference was scheduled. At this point, Mateo's parents just wanted to hear any encouraging news about their son's progress. It pleased them to hear Mateo's teacher say that she had started using iPads for certain lessons. This meant Mateo could type information instead of writing it on a worksheet, and he could also use apps for practicing various skills.

It was a small step, but Mateo's parents were encouraged. Right before the conference ended, however, Mateo's teacher asked if his parents had viewed her classroom blog lately. They had, and as they spoke about a particular video clip of the holiday program rehearsal, Mateo's dad realized why the teacher had brought it up. The clip showed Mateo dancing off to the side as the other children went through the motions exactly as they had been instructed.

The entire conversation turned to, "Which kid is not like the others?" Mateo's parents were horrified that his teacher saw anything *different* as *bad* and needing correction. This occurrence became a catalyst for change in the way Mateo's parents handled school matters for their son. They became determined never to allow anyone to make their son feel ashamed. They wanted him to feel cherished and supported in his education.

After the meeting, Mateo's parents reflected on what their family had experienced and emailed their thoughts to the principal because it was important that every team member responsible for Mateo's education help him be more successful and reach his potential. They began by outlining what *they* would do as parents. Their home-based strategies included:

- Giving positive feedback for progress.
- Breaking assignments into smaller, achievable tasks.
- Not punishing Mateo for incomplete schoolwork.
- Implementing tactile techniques for spelling and using more online modules for math practice.

Then they outlined what they felt the *school* should do for their son. They requested that:

- School work should be reasonably tailored so Mateo could manage each assignment.
- Mateo would be accountable for any behaviors that distracted other children from learning, but not be punished for not finishing work when he tried his best.
- Unfinished work would be sent home so the parents could determine if the assignment was about a skill he needed to learn or just about finishing a paper. If it was the latter, he would

not finish the homework. (Example: A math homework page might have twenty problems to complete. Mateo could solve ten correctly without help, so his parents did not require him to finish the entire page. He exhibited he had mastered the math skill on his homework.)

- Mateo would receive encouraging feedback in the form of positive notes and stickers on classwork when he showed any improvements or even small steps toward improvements.
- The teacher would never again videotape a child with the intention of shaming him.

After the bumpy ride in second grade, I felt Mateo's parents needed a support group or someone else who understood their situation. I arranged a coffee date with another mother with a 2e son whose journey had been remarkably like Mateo's. The two women made an instant connection. Mateo's mother no longer felt alone. She had another parent who did not judge her or Mateo, but instead helped her navigate the potential obstacles that were to come as Mateo progressed in school.

One would think, after the unfair challenges in Mateo's second grade experience, that there would not be many success stories to tell. However, by the end of second grade, he was making progress in several areas.

This progress was brought about by the changes both in school and at home. First, Mateo's teacher came to realize that there were other ways her students could practice skills and be assessed without using traditional paper and pencil tasks. She also began to write positive comments on all students' papers if they made even the slightest progress on something that challenged them.

Mateo's parents helped him learn to adapt to more structure, too. They established a homework routine, provided a homework-friendly area with supplies, kept distractions to a minimum, offered praise, and arranged small breaks if necessary. As they changed the way they helped their son complete his homework, Mateo's frustration levels declined significantly. His self-confidence improved because he was finishing work that usually took him hours to complete. Finally, Mateo seemed to regain his excitement about school. He looked forward to third grade and talked about how he was going to get better at following directions and finishing his work on time.

Here is a note from Mateo's Second Grade Teacher.

> *I thought as an educator who had over 35 years of experience teaching, I had worked with every type of student imaginable. However, when I met Mateo, I discovered I was wrong. He presented a unique set of challenges for me as a teacher. My perception of gifted children was based on some students I had instructed several years before working with Mateo. They were very smart, and I had to work hard to keep them challenged. At the time, I did not know that smart children could also have learning disorders or have challenges with age-appropriate skills.*
>
> *It was always in my nature to try to have a student fit my teaching style. I never stopped to think that many of my students did not fulfill their potential because they were not instructed in a way that matched their special needs and learning styles. However, after teaching Mateo, I knew I had to change the way I taught my students. I realized I had to do a better job of being part of an instructional team with parents and other specialists.*
>
> *After so many years of teaching, I thought I knew best. But after working with Mateo, I could see his parents were true advocates for their son and nothing would stand in their way to make sure he reached his potential. Working collaboratively always seemed to get the best results. I know I am a better teacher now after working with Mateo and his family.*

Third Grade

After his unpleasant second-grade year, Mateo's family made a conscious effort to relax and enjoy every moment of summer vacation. Besides visiting the public library for new books each week, the only school-related task Mateo engaged was working with an occupational therapist to improve his writing. Mateo's parents understood that they would have to continue being their son's number one advocates and communicate often and openly with school staff about his needs.

As summer ended and third grade approached, Mateo's parents bolstered his confidence by telling him it would be a great year because they had met his new teacher and liked her very much. They were not surprised when Mateo described his class as enjoyable. His teacher smiled a lot, and she let the students move around the room.

As winter break approached, Mateo's parents expressed that they were more comfortable with conferences because they felt no one was finger-pointing and everyone had the same objective: to shine a positive light on Mateo's many strengths and support his area of need. Everyone was optimistic, and it showed in the progress Mateo was making in school.

In February, students were preparing to take grade level achievement tests. Prior to third grade, Mateo's scores had always been lower than his parents expected. However, they felt this was because he had trouble focusing on a given task for an extended period, and academic testing requires children to sit quietly and focus without being able to ask their teacher questions. However, by mid-week, Mateo mentioned to his mother he felt stressed about having to complete so many tests. At one point, Mateo randomly filled in the test bubbles without giving them any thought at all. His teacher stopped him because he said he was tired of trying. After some kind words of encouragement, Mateo resumed the testing.

This situation provided an excellent opportunity for Mateo's parents to impart a valuable lesson to their son. They discussed with him that everyone faces demanding times and must persist to be successful. The word *perseverance* became a friendly school and household word used to encourage children to strive to do their best regardless of the challenge set before them.[82]

This year, it was clear that the caring team who helped Mateo made an impact. No one wanted to "fix" him. Instead, teachers and adults helped him set achievable goals so his successes would propel him forward. Mateo ended third grade with enthusiasm and excitement for his journey in fourth grade. Finally, this smart boy had learned it was all right to learn differently than others. Mateo also realized he would always get hugs and encouragement from his family for being exactly who he was.

I interviewed Mateo when he was in third grade and and these are some of his insights about himself and his schooling. Mateo was very comfortable talking to me about his experiences in school because he felt I understood and supported him. If all his teachers got to know him like I did, they would appreciate all his qualities, not just the ones that made their job easier.

Mateo's Reflections.

If you met me, you might describe me as silly and funny. Sometimes I have a bad temper, though I enjoy being creative. I know a lot about animals and living things. I enjoy video games, puzzles, and some reading. I like playing with my friends, swimming, and playing basketball. I know I am smart, but when I heard the word gifted for the first time, I wasn't sure what it meant.

I sort of like school. Sometimes it is hard for me and sometimes it is easy. When it is hard, I feel like I don't belong. For example, during grammar lessons, I struggle to understand some things my teacher has taught. It is then I don't feel very smart. It seems everyone else is better at this subject than me. The worst part of school is taking tests. I get frustrated trying to finish and get everything right. But I do try my best.

School seems to be easiest for me when I have a teacher who is nice. First grade was easy for me because I had a teacher I liked, and she helped me. Second grade was difficult because I had a very strict teacher. She made me feel out of place at times.

I felt better about third grade than second grade. My teacher didn't make me feel like I was supposed to be perfect. In third grade, I was also allowed to move around more in the classroom. Sometimes I even sat on a big round ball instead of a regular chair. This helped me, because if I sat for too long, I got wiggly. The ball chair allowed me to move while I was sitting.

When I think about what I liked in third grade, I think about playing math games, finding a series of books I enjoyed and being with friends. My gifted classes are cool. I like that there are not many kids in this class and my teacher can spend time helping me understand what we are learning. We worked on activities that made me happy.

Something else I remember about third grade was I started taking medicine to help me focus in class. My medicine helped me finish my work. Before, it took me a long time to complete one assignment. I felt much better about myself at the end of third grade.

My family helps me with school. They help with homework and studying for tests, especially spelling tests. My dad reads books with me and then quizzes me about them. I think my best subject in school is science. I always enjoy projects related to animals and other science topics.

Mateo is now in upper elementary school and making good progress. His parents continue to be strong advocates for him, and his teachers provide support with organizational help and accommodations in writing.

Mateo is also learning to type, and he takes pride in his schoolwork. All in all, Mateo's bumpy beginning in school has been replaced with a steadier, happier road trip.

In the 'road trip' assistance table blow, teachers and parents will see examples of problems that students like Mateo may experience in school. Once the problems are identified, then a map or plan is created by the teacher, parent, or both to resolve each type of problem. Ultimately, the goal is to help the 2e student find a more meaningful journey in school and accept himself, without feeling he is somehow broken and needs to be "fixed."

Table 4.1. Road Trip Assistance for Students Like Mateo

Roadblock	RoadMap	Destination
Teachers collect only quantifiable (formal assessments) measures in school to review students' progress. Instruction and interventions are limited.	• Teachers collect both quantifiable and qualitative data (observations) to inform instructions and interventions for all students.	• Quantitative and qualitative student data offers teachers an efficient, objective way to create more personalized learning experiences, create more effective lesson plans, and offer students the best chance to succeed.
Students' behaviors and performances in school confuse teachers. ("Can this kid be gifted?") *Examples*: • Students need to organize people and things (seen as bossy.) • Intense feelings (seen as immature.) • Imaginational overexcitability (seen as daydreaming.) • Psychomotor overexcitability seen as ADHD.	• Teachers *will* be trained to recognize and meet the needs of advanced students. • Gifted specialists become part of the teaching team.	• Teachers respond to individual student strengths and make referrals for further assessments where appropriate. • Identified gifted students receive support services from trained specialists. • Gifted specialists support regular classroom teachers.

Teachers and parents are perplexed that some gifted students' cognitive abilities and school performances are uneven or "out-of-sync."	Teacher/parent workshops and other gifted education resources: • Dispel myths about gifted children. • Provide information on 2e students and asynchronous development.	Teachers and parents: • Learn to appreciate that not all smart children perform or behave the same. • Recognize some gifted children have learning disabilities. • Manage expectations-both their own and those of others.
Gifted students are placed with incompatible and inflexible teachers.	Teachers and parents: • Include gifted interventionists as part of teams to plan for students. • Build collaborative relationships to avoid large-scale problems.	• Teachers consider learning styles of all students. • Classroom teachers, specialists, and parents work as educational teams for children's best interests.
Students with asynchronous development experience self-esteem problems.	Teachers and parents: • Learn which areas of development are out of sync to better determine educational plan for child (physical, social, emotional).	• With support and maturation, students begin to "balance."

Twice-exceptional students are punished for their differences and left vulnerable.	Teachers and parents use accommodations to empower children, not control them. These include: • Developing gifts and talents with opportunities including advanced classes in talent areas, working on creative projects with other talented students, mentorships, and competitions. • Using activities that engage children, such as project-based learning and creative problem solving. • Placing 2e students with others who share their interests and skills to maximize attention and learning.	Students: • Embrace their own differences. • Gain confidence they can succeed. • Develop optimally.
Students rarely see positive feedback on their classwork.	Teachers: • Provide constructive feedback in the form of encouraging notes, stickers, oral praise, and emails to families.	Students: • Reflect on their achievements. • Continue to make progress in school.
School-to-home communications display student in negative manner.	Teachers: • Post only positive student achievements in emails, blogs, and bulletin board displays.	• All students feel encouraged to provide their best efforts on school assignments.

Parents struggle with decision to medicate children with ADHD diagnoses.	• Conversations with pediatricians, counselors, psychologists help families understand positive and negative aspects of using medication for treating ADHD.	• With the help of their doctors and other experts, families make the best decisions for their children regarding the use of medications.
Students have limited focus.	Strategies are implemented to help students focus: • Stress balls • Sensory fidget toys • Bouncy bands on chair legs • Check lists • Study carrels • Therapy ball seats • Movement breaks	• Students can relieve excess energy with the use of specific strategies and tools. • Number of completed class and homework assignments increases.
Students' frustration with school-wide achievement tests cause: • Students to randomly select answers. • Discrepancies between test results and students' abilities.	Teachers and parents: • Teach students relaxation techniques, especially for test days. • Teach students persistence so they can work through challenges. • Carefully monitor students on testing days. • Prepare students for what to expect on testing days.	Students: • Best efforts reveal their true abilities. • Achieve goals they have set for themselves.

Chapter 5
Jamal's Story: Gifted with ADHD and Obsessive-Compulsive Disorder

(Note: Although it is unusual for a child to be diagnosed with OCD by second grade, Jamal's parents sought help from a child psychologist when they noticed very early in their son's life, he had unwanted thoughts and fears that caused anxiety. For example, he felt his food had bugs in it so the ritual of seeing how his parents prepared his food or by having food cut into little, tiny pieces helped him feel okay. After several interviews with Jamal and his parents, including the completion of checklists and questionnaires, the psychologist diagnosed Jamal with Obsessive Compulsive Disorder.)

Getting to Know My Student

Jamal was an unhappy boy when I first met him in second grade. One reason was that he had to leave behind the beloved school (it had closed) he had attended for kindergarten and first grade. Jamal was also shy and sensitive. He had great difficulty adjusting to new environments and people.

Jamal had already been identified as gifted at his previous school. So, I began working with him right away in our gifted groups. At the beginning of each class, I asked students to share some happy news about their lives, and I usually heard about new pets, birthday parties, and grandparent visits. But when it came time for Jamal to share happy news, he responded by looking at the table and saying, "I don't have any happy news." This went on for weeks.

One day I noticed Jamal drawing a picture as a part of a project in our class. It was extremely detailed. One of his classmates told Jamal he liked the drawing because it looked real. It was at that moment the "ice" broke, and Jamal began to feel comfortable with his peers. He was not only very smart, but he was a talented artist. Each time the subject of drawing was mentioned, Jamal lit up like a Christmas tree. Art was his comfort zone, and he could talk about it for hours.

Because Jamal was extremely sensitive to almost everything in his life, the decisions he made were to protect his own feelings. Once he said to me, "I like to use big words when I speak and write, but I don't use them at school because others will make fun of me." This comment made me realize how important it was for Jamal to learn to accept himself as a very smart boy who was different from his regular classroom peers. With support from his peers and teachers, Jamal became more comfortable in his own skin. He let others see him without a "mask" and he no longer feared being judged by others. Finally, he began to share "happy news" to his classes and at home.

Parenting Jamal

> *"The trick to raising a gifted child is to find that all-around balance."*
>
> ~Jamal's mother

Like many parents of gifted children, Jamal's parents saw a few early indicators their son was bright. "He started to talk at the age of one," his mother said. "Once it started, he took off. By the time he was 18 months old, he had a vocabulary of about 200 words. Our son was always interested in books. We read to him all the time."

I often hear this kind of story when I speak to parents of high-potential children. However, the difference with Jamal was that once he started pre-school, he also had some behavior issues that overshadowed his high ability. His teachers discussed testing him for learning disabilities, including autism. They never suggested Jamal might be gifted.

However, a bell went off when Jamal took a plane trip with his mother. A fellow passenger on the flight overheard Jamal and his mother speaking. She told Jamal's mother she was a gifted specialist and felt he exhibited signs of giftedness. Jamal's parents always thought their son was very smart, but they waited until first grade to have him tested. It was then he was identified as highly gifted.

As an observant parent, Jamal's mother noticed her son enjoyed drawing very much, but he held his pencil in his fist. Once he stared kindergarten and learned how to hold a pencil correctly, his drawing ability took off.

Attention Deficit Hyperactivity Disorder

While he was in kindergarten, Jamal's teacher and mother noticed he struggled socially, trailed behind his peers in fine motor skills, and was very sensitive to textures. In first grade, Jamal displayed difficulty following instructions, organizing simple tasks, failed to finish some schoolwork, and had trouble staying seated. Although many young children experience these behaviors when they start school, Jamal's behaviors were more extreme. Fortunately, Jamal's proactive parents sought the advice of a qualified psychologist who worked with gifted children.

When further screening was completed by the psychologist, Jamal's parents' intuition that their son had ADHD was proven correct. They were relieved in many ways with this diagnosis because they felt they could now focus on strategies that could help this 2e boy.

Note: It is often difficult to make the correct diagnosis with young children. Many gifted children (including twice-exceptional) seem to be misdiagnosed because so few health professionals receive any training about giftedness. The characteristics of a gifted child may appear to be a disorder, such as extreme sensitivity and over-excitability. Jamal's parents were correct to seek the advice of a psychologist who was trained to understand gifted children. He provided a thorough examination of the facts in this child's case before a diagnosis was given. I would direct all parents to access the SENG Misdiagnosis Initiative at http://sengifted.org/programs/misdiagnosis-initiative for more information on this important topic.

Many professionals like educators, psychologists and pediatricians don't feel it necessary to test students for what they categorize as general behavioral concerns that could be managed in the class and at home with behavioral therapy techniques. However, parents' intuition is often precisely on target. Jamal's parents went to work researching ways to help their son at home, and they also wanted Jamal's school to write an intervention plan to support his twice-exceptionality. Without it, they knew he would not grow academically, socially, and emotionally. Many families don't want to put labels on their kids, but Jamal's parents understood this kind of intervention was important for their son to make progress. Unless he was formally identified as twice-exceptional, they felt teachers might overlook either his giftedness or his learning disability. Either way, Jamal would fall behind and be in jeopardy of not reaching his potential.

They felt fortunate to be able to read and discuss advanced topics such as science, politics, or current events with their child. Some gifted children enjoy going with their parents to interesting lectures, watching education programs, or visiting museums, activities that an average elementary student might find boring or uninteresting. Jamal particularly enjoyed the local science center because he would move freely through the exhibits, always revisiting the ones that were of high interest to him. Sharing these elevated learning experiences with their child is fun for parents, too.

However, the other side of giftedness is that families often deal with childhood concerns others don't experience. Some gifted children question everything to the point of exhausting their family members. Some are highly anxious. No matter how their parents and teachers comfort and reassure them, their worry and anxiety doesn't let up. They have trouble making friends, so socializing with other children is hard. Even at social gatherings, the child may gravitate to adults for conversation.

Jamal exhibited all of these traits. First, when he discovered a topic of interest, he questioned everyone with great intensity about it. He also had to find 'every' book about the topic and do all his own investigation. These activities could go on for weeks.

Obsessive-Compulsive Disorder

Note: "Obsessions are intrusive unwanted thoughts or images that can cause significant distress and anxiety."[83]

Jamal was anxious, both at home and at school. He worried about things that his peers didn't even consider. For example, if his teacher did not smile much throughout the day, Jamal thought she didn't like him. Jamal's mother said there was a time when he would not eat apples because he feared worms. Unless the fruit was cut open and he could see inside, he refused to eat it. These behaviors caused Jamal to have few friends. She arranged a play date for Jamal, and it went well, or so she thought. But when she tried to call the mother of the other boy to arrange a second play date, this parent declined the invitation for unexplained reasons.

In second grade, Jamal's parents arranged for their son to work with a specialist who provided treatments in the form of behavior therapy for his OCD. "Behavior therapy can help the child change negative thoughts into more positive, effective ways of thinking, leading to more effective behavior."[84] With help from Jamal's therapist, Jamal's mother gradually exposed her son to his fears in the safety of their home. She would examine apples with Jamal and point out there were no holes in the apples for worms. They would cut them open and discover it was true. This exercise helped Jamal significantly decrease his anxiety because this scientific and practical approach was more understandable than anxiety.

Gifted children may demand a great deal of time and attention. Jamal's family always found time to sit and discuss their son's many ideas and questions. It was also important to make extensive visits to the library and investigate specialized camps to nurture Jamal's interests.

Jamal's parents were well aware that not everyone understood what it was like to rear a gifted boy, particularly one with disabilities. Often, they heard parents talk about how great it would be to have a smart kid who did well in school. Their reality, though, was that it was difficult raising Jamal in a society where people want to help children who struggle with learning disabilities, but don't understand that talented and gifted children, especially ones with emotional challenges like Jamal, need extra help and understanding as well. Like Mateo's family, Jamal's parents were very disappointed to see a double standard at work, offering special education students expanded resources and special teachers, while gifted students do not receive this equally deserved extra care.

When they realized that Jamal's second grade teacher lacked compassion and understanding, they became determined to educate others about the need to support 2e students without bias. Jamal's mother explained that she would advocate for her son by educating all his teachers about the need for remediation, as well as the need for opportunities to promote her son's individual strengths and talents. This parent was her child's best advocate in school.

Jamal's parents did not leave anything to chance when it came to their son's education. Before he began kindergarten, they observed several schools they considered good matches for Jamal's needs. They ultimately chose a warm and inviting school in which they felt all children could flourish.

When Jamal began kindergarten, his mother described their son's teacher as kind but strict, with definite expectations for her students. She was fair and did not pick favorites. She used music to bring calm energy to the classroom. Classroom management was one of her strengths. Jamal's parents were pleased with how well things went that year.

They described Jamal's first grade teacher as young, positive, and fun. She was extremely supportive of each child's needs. A huge bonus for Jamal this year was that his teacher appreciated his creativity and encouraged it. Everyone was happy to be at this school, and it showed in each child's daily progress.

Unfortunately, due to low enrollment, Jamal's wonderful school had to close. His family got the disappointing news at the end of his first-grade year. Jamal's mother made an appointment to visit a nearby school with a good academic reputation. It had been honored as a "National Blue-Ribbon School" for exemplary achievement-and it had a gifted program. After the principal gave her a tour and satisfactorily answered her questions regarding Jamal's special needs, she enrolled him in second grade.

He struggled most of the year because it seemed that his teacher focused on areas of weakness instead of promoting his areas of strength. Jamal felt she was punitive and harsh. This attitude could be traced to her lack of knowledge about his special needs. Once she discovered the issues, which were ADHD and anxiety, she was able to work with the Intervention Assistance Team (IAT) to provide appropriate accommodations for Jamal.

Jamal's third grade year proceeded without major roadblocks because his teacher understood giftedness, ADHD, and OCD, and how each one affected a student's performance in school. She supported each child with positive feedback about their strengths and areas of need. However, after the third grade, Jamal's parents felt he required daily support for the social and emotional aspects of growing up gifted. Twice-a-week gifted classes were not enough for his special challenges. Jamal's mother felt that if she did not find help for her son in areas such as making friends, managing perfectionism, and the need to advance in areas of strength, Jamal might have bigger issues to grapple with as he got older.

She felt if he stayed in his current school, he might become isolated or lose his creativity because he felt he needed to conform to be accepted. It was the parents' wish that Jamal would come home excited about school five days a week, rather than only the days he met with his gifted classmates. Seeing their son overcome challenges while working with his gifted peers prompted their decision to find a school where Jamal could work all week with teachers trained in gifted education and students who had similar needs.

His parents decided to transfer Jamal to a gifted academy for fourth grade. This school's mission included a curriculum with the appropriate acceleration and differentiation options to address the varied needs of the students and to serve the social and emotional needs of gifted children. They felt it was fortunate to have found such a school.

Teaching Jamal

Second Grade

Jamal was seven years old and in the second grade when I met him. His parents stated he was a strong reader and had been identified as 2e, gifted with attention deficit disorder and obsessive-compulsive disorder.

As I began my observations of Jamal in his second-grade room, I became concerned. First, he was extremely unhappy. He had several meltdowns throughout the day, lots of unfinished work, and no real desire to even want to be in school and make new friends. His teacher and I discussed whether he needed more time for the transition to his new school, or whether there was a bigger concern we were not yet aware of.

Jamal's mother had described her son as having a love of learning. She was surprised he was struggling to adjust to his new school environment. His teacher and I mentioned, however, that Jamal did not complete his class work on a regular basis. It took him twice as long to finish an assignment as it did the other children. He also did not like working with his classmates. If cooperative group work was arranged, he continually asked if he could work alone. Finally, Jamal took almost ten minutes after entering class in the morning to put away his coat, book bag, snack, and homework because he wanted it done in a very specific way. This caused his entire day to be affected because he could never seem to catch up. The classroom teacher and I were perplexed, and we hoped Jamal's parents could shed some light on why their son seemed so unhappy. We decide to have an early parent-teacher conference.

What We Learned

During the conference, Jamal's parents said their son was emotional and intense and showed signs of obsessive-compulsive disorder. This added complexity to the situation since Jamal had been diagnosed with ADHD and OCD in first grade.

As the meeting neared an end, we received information we wished we had known about before school began. In first grade Jamal had a 504 Plan, which is "developed to ensure that a child who has a disability under the law and is attending an elementary or secondary educational institution receives accommodations that will ensure their academic success and access to the learning environment."[85] His mother said her son made huge strides when small changes were made to his learning environment. With this information, we made changes to help this smart boy succeed.

Together with the school's Intervention Assistance Team, which consisted of the principal, a counselor, parents, interventionists, and the classroom teacher, a plan was constructed that addressed the issues holding Jamal back. He needed accommodations to address his ADHD, OCD, giftedness, and introversion.

Jamal had tried hard in school, but he had walked into a new environment where no one knew his special needs. In addition, because he was shy, he never asked for help. The IAT agreed that we would start with only two goals: time management; and strategies to help Jamal handle his anxiety. With improvement in these two areas, the team felt Jamal also would experience success in many other aspects of his school experience.

Time Management Strategies

Within the first few weeks of school, Jamal's teacher and I noticed that he had to make sure each letter he wrote was perfect. Sometimes he even felt the need to retrace certain letters. When this happened, especially during spelling tests and other written work, he needed twice as much time as other students to finish. We suggested he use an iPad or the class computer for these tasks. He was happy to have this option because he was already learning to use a keyboard.

Jamal's other teachers (for art, music, and technology) applied time management strategies in their classes as well. Simply breaking projects into smaller parts and setting a timer for completion was all that we needed to keep Jamal on task, as well as most of the other children in his classes.

Tips for Teaching Kids Time Management Age-by-Age[86]

Pre-schoolers Age 3-4	**Talk about the changing of seasons.** • Observing a tree over seasons is a tangible representation of the passage of time. • Create a picture schedule. • The preschool world uses visual cues to help young children keep on track. It provides them with order and predictability. • Practice waiting. • Time management is a skill linked to better study habits and grades. Young children can practice marking off a special event on a calendar as it gets closer.
Kindergarten through Second Grade Ages 5-7	**Find a Place for Everything** • Organization must come before time management. Children are encouraged to keep their homework supplies organized. **Use a Visual Timer** • Apps like *Children's Countdown* and *Timer* help children tackle their assignment more effectively and efficiently.
Third to Fifth Grade Ages 8-10	**Work on Estimating Time** • Students can make their own schedules, but they need a good sense of how long things take. Practice with homework and extracurricular activities. **Plan for Long Term Assignments** • Long range projects need to be broken down into smaller steps. Use sticky notes on a calendar in case tasks have to move to another day. **Set Priorities** • Students need to understand the difference between "have to" and "want to" in order to prioritize and self-monitor.

Issues with Anxiety

Jamal's teacher and I knew that movement was going to be a key factor in preventing or reducing anxious moments in his day. Sandra Rief explains in her book *How to reach and teach children with ADD/ADHD* that exercise provides individuals with ADHD an outlet to expend excess energy, while increasing the enzymes in the brain that are responsible for learning and memory.[87] Jamal was given special permission to leave the room and take short walks in the hall if he became overly stressed. He also had a piece of Velcro placed inside his desk that he could rub when he felt anxious. He liked it because it was inconspicuous and helped him calm down. He said it felt like stroking a cat.

Jamal became anxious in working with other students because he felt they were judging him. I was not surprised to see this happen because gifted children with intensity and heightened sensitivities often experience anxiety.[88] He was uncomfortable sharing his authentic self with anyone and said he felt his teacher wanted him to be like everyone else. This concerned him because he knew he was different from his peers.

To support Jamal, I worked with him in my gifted classes helping him research smart people who also grew up feeling different. When he discovered that many successful people had once experienced the same feelings he had, Jamal began to enjoy sharing with others. I also supported his regular classroom teacher and her lessons regarding how we are all unique and we each need to be valued and respected by our peers.

Introversion

Many gifted young people are introverts.[89] This does not mean they are misfits who lack social skills. The major difference between introverts and extroverts is not whether they have the ability to get along with others; some introverts do that well. What differentiates the two groups is that introverts draw their energy from being alone with themselves, whereas extroverts draw energy from being with others. Schools, in general, are set up for extroverts and can be loud, crowded, overstimulating environments focused on action rather than reflection.[90] These overwhelming characteristics can make learning harder for introverts.

Many introverts are also highly sensitive, said Susan Cain in her groundbreaking book *Quiet: The Power of Introverts in a World That Can't Stop Talking.*[91] Jamal's high sensitivity made school more of a challenge for him. For students like Jamal, too much stimulation is exhausting. Journaling, artistic pursuits, and working alone give them time to recuperate from long periods of group work, noise, and confusion.

Table 5.1. Introverts and Extroverts[92]

Introverts	Extroverts
Desire private space/time	Are social animals
Become drained around large groups of people: dislike attending large gatherings	Like being around lots of other people, become more and more stimulated in the presence of others
Prefer to work on own rather than in a group	Like work groups where they can try out many different ideas and enjoy lots of conversation
Are cautious about meeting people, although they may disguise this well and sometimes seem to be extroverts	Meet and converse with others easily
Form a few deep attachments. May take time to warm up and show their real selves to others	Have many friends and talk to them for long periods of time. Share personal information easily

No one is a pure introvert or extrovert. All of us fall along a continuum and exhibit some of the traits of each type. Extroverts can sometimes be unsure and shy, while introverts may be good at leading a group. Introversion is not a weakness, and introverts often have outstanding problem-solving abilities. It's important to listen to the class introverts as well as to the children who constantly have their hands in the air.

By mid-year, Jamal had made incredible growth on his 504 Plan. His morning routine had been accomplished, and he started his bell work, the first task of the class period, without reminders. Jamal also completed more daily assignments with the help of technology, and he began participating in more class discussions and small group projects. He realized his classmates would not make fun of him for his advanced vocabulary, and they enjoyed learning about new topics from him. Jamal made connections with a couple of boys in his class because they shared some interests. Overall, his confidence grew, and he was more comfortable showing the class the "real" Jamal. His teacher and I were happy he had decided not to hide his intelligence anymore.

At the end of second grade, Jamal's parents and the IAT met to review his 504 Plan. We agreed that our smart boy had met his two goals on many levels. He was no longer drifting aimlessly or experiencing meltdowns because he was lost. His teachers understood his needs and supported them with appropriate strategies. Jamal was smiling often now because he had made strides with his writing and his peer interactions. He still experienced anxiety from time to time, but it was manageable. This smart boy had finally let his guard down and allowed others into his world. When his classroom teacher asked if he needed any extra help with an assignment, Jamal often responded, "No, I think I'm all right."

As we planned for the next year, we established a new 504 Plan, making sure to include in the process his specially selected third-grade teacher. She participated fully in creating several new goals for him. The summer was an enjoyable one for Jamal because potential roadblocks to his success had been removed.

Third Grade

Jamal entered third grade feeling better about himself, and his new teacher was aware of his strengths and areas of need as the first day of school approached.

When Jamal's new school scheduled their open house for students to meet their teachers and bring their school supplies, his teacher recommended that Jamal and his mother come a little earlier than the scheduled time. She knew he might be overwhelmed by the noise and crowds of a traditional open house. Jamal's mother appreciated this option and the teacher's thoughtfulness. After this initial meeting, Jamal could go home and process what his new room looked like, where he would be sitting, and who his teacher would be. All of these activities were helpful to an introvert like Jamal, who needed to have time alone or with his parents, or to digest what he had seen and heard. Although most students are anxious about starting a new school year, Jamal's increased intensity about new situations was eased with a simple one-on-one meeting with a kind and accommodating teacher.

Although Jamal was prepared academically, the transition to a new grade level was intensified for him because he still had a multitude of questions. He worried about his need to move around in a classroom, peer relationships, and getting all of his work done on time. He still reflected on his often-painful experiences in second grade and fretted about whether he would have the same ones in the new classroom.

As school got under way, Jamal's teacher observed he was very quiet in class. This concerned her for many reasons. She wanted him to make friends and feel included in student conversations and activities. It was also important for Jamal to participate in class discussions because he had a lot to offer. If he was withdrawn and afraid to speak to his classmates, he could get lost quickly.

Fortunately, the teacher's ability to develop a positive classroom culture in which she provided choices, asked students for their input, and encouraged them to interact with her and each other allowed Jamal to see that he was in a safe environment.

Jamal's teacher had been assigned the gifted third grade cluster group of students. Being in the cluster group and enjoying a more relaxed environment did wonders for Jamal. He also benefited from flexible grouping for specific projects, during which he interacted with all the members of the class and learned to enjoy their company.

Nonetheless, Jamal still struggled with some stress and tension. As he said to his mother, "No one has compulsions or anxiety like I do." I mentioned to her I had read stories to my class about famous gifted people who struggled in school and sometimes life, but who had succeeded despite their problems. I recommended she do the same at home. When Jamal read about gifted men like Edison and Einstein, who likely were twice-exceptional, he realized he wasn't alone. This helped him let his guard down a bit more.

The classroom teacher and I also felt it might be a good time to reintroduce the option of carrying a "squishy ball" or "stress ball" for those times anxiety seemed to creep up. (These are small balls or objects filled with malleable gel or foam that are held in the palm of the hand. The act of repeatedly squeezing the ball releases tension and relieves stress.) In second grade, Jamal did not like this idea because he felt he would have to explain to others why he was holding it, and this made him feel different from the other students. But now when his teacher gave him one to try, he politely accepted it. He was no longer concerned about others asking him why he carried it to all his classes. After a few days of using the stress ball, he realized very few kids were even interested. This experience taught Jamal he was not being judged by the other kids, and that things he worried about sometimes never came to fruition.

Jamal's parents, teacher, and I felt that third grade was an altogether better experience than second grade had been. The reason was twofold. First, Jamal's parents were proactive, and they requested a 504 Plan be in place before third grade began. Second, the third-grade teacher never tried to "fix" anyone. In other words, she embraced Jamal's differences, and this attitude allowed him to show his authentic self to those around him.

Nonetheless, despite the accommodations the school had made for Jamal, his parents were still concerned about his overall feelings that he didn't fit into his school. They researched other educational alternatives for him, located a gifted academy close to their home, and visited several times before school dismissed for the summer.

A major advantage to this nearby gifted academy was that its curriculum included daily attention to social and emotional needs of their students. Another was that the entire teaching staff had specialized training in working with gifted children. When Jamal told his parents he was comfortable transferring to the gifted academy, they made the arrangements. I was sad to see Jamal leave, but I applauded his parents for being his strongest advocates and seeking the best educational fit for him so he could continue to make progress academically, socially, and emotionally.

A Note from Jamal's Third Grade Teacher:

Jamal was a very bright student in my class. Although he did not participate in group conversations in the beginning of the year, he soon warmed up to the class routine and dynamics. My class this year was friendly, and all the students supported each other regardless of differences. I observed Jamal having some bad days, but most were good ones. On his bad days, I could see he would have preferred to stay home instead of coming to school. He liked to carry his stress ball everywhere he went.

I could tell Jamal had made progress when I witnessed that he felt comfortable enough in class to use his extensive vocabulary without feeling as though others were judging him. Jamal brought many talents to our room. He simply loved to read and share his knowledge about snakes and Egypt, to name a few. When I saw Jamal's drawings for the first time, I was astounded at the details he included in each one. Drawing seemed to take him to a place where he felt totally relaxed and appreciated. I will be surprised if illustrating is not part of his career someday.

Jamal's Reflections:

I would describe myself as smart and cheerful. I'm also kind, thoughtful, and considerate. I'm creative because I think up plans for movies, inventions, and things that help people. When I have free time, I enjoy reading, playing with Legos and video games, and drawing. I also do what I call "explosions." I jump around and pretend to be in stories. The more hyper I am, the more role playing I can experience.

School can be challenging for me because it requires a lot of concentration. Second grade was the most difficult year because I felt like my teacher tried to make me fit into a box. But I am unique, and I discovered that I needed to be educated differently from most of my classmates. My enjoyment for school was lost in second grade when I felt like I had to do lots of repetitive paperwork. There were times I felt my teacher was impatient with me. This made me feel stressed.

> *In school, I knew my strengths were reading, Earth science, grammar, and social studies. I'm always curious and constantly active. I think it's important for people to know that gifted children have weaknesses, too. I am not great at math, but I think I'm okay. I have trouble paying attention and following directions on paperwork. I sometimes skim through my work, not doing my best. I also try to cram too much detail into things like artwork or stories. Finally, my handwriting is messy, and I know that bothers some of my teachers. But learning how to use an iPad and computer helped me with this part of school.*

A note: Both Jamal and Mateo were diagnosed with ADHD. Mateo required medication, but the accommodations made for Jamal were sufficient for him to move on in school, sometimes with difficulty, but without medication. Even children with ADHD are different from one another, and the decisions surrounding this diagnosis must be carefully thought out.

The road trip assistance chart for students like Jamal guides teachers and parents to work together to identify the roadblocks that keep the child moving forward in school and life. Children with more than one disability, combined with their giftedness, often find themselves totally lost in school. They require the immediate attention of caring adults to unlock their potential and get them moving again.

Table 5.2. Road Trip Assistance for Students like Jamal

Roadblock	RoadMap	Destination
New students arrive at schools with limited records.	**Parents:** • Provide schools with children's medical histories and any previous Individual Education Plans (IEP) or 504 Plans. **School:** • Create collaborative teams (teachers, specialists, parents) to support students with special needs. • Collect additional data to assess students' needs.	• New data reveals some students are twice-exceptional. • Appropriate educational plans are written for 2e students.

Students experience anxiety disorders or panic attacks, resulting in poor relationships with peers and difficulty managing classroom demands.	**Teachers/parents:** • Help children discover triggers for anxieties (i.e., thoughts, people, objects, situations). • Teach relaxation/coping strategies and techniques.[93] • Express positive, but realistic expectations. • Enhance learning environment.[94] • Seek additional professional evaluations/support (counselors/therapists)	• Proactive measures help students manage anxieties.
Students have difficulties completing multistep assignments and/ or projects on a timeline.	**Teachers/parents:** • Break assignments into manageable/achievable parts. • Extend time to complete work. • Provide direct instruction in organization, time management, and study skills.	• Students experience success in completing longer assignments. • Self-esteem improves.
Students experience pain, strain, and/or discomfort writing. **Students:** • Assignments are illegible. • Are resistant to finishing work. • Write too slowly or too fast.	**Teachers/parents:** • Teach word processing skills. • Decrease quantity of writing. • Dictate or record assignments. • Provide flexibility/choice in activities. • Call on specialists, such as occupational therapists. **Students:** • Try assorted pencil grips. • Explore various writing instruments (pens, markers). • Try modified pencils such as a *Twist-N- Write* or a *Lyra Ferby*. • Take frequent breaks.	**Students:** • Negative attitudes about writing change to positive ones. • Handwriting improves. • Self-efficacy is boosted.

<table>
<tr>
<td>Students are slow completing classroom and home routines.</td>
<td>Students (with parents'/ teachers' help):<ul><li>Predict time task will take to complete.</li><li>Practice "beat your best time" game/log results.</li><li>Prioritize tasks.</li><li>Check completed tasks off list.</li></ul></td>
<td><ul><li>Students continue to work towards their "personal best" times completing routines.</li><li>Adults and students observe improvements with task completions at home and school.</li><li>Independence is achieved completing school and home routines.</li></ul></td>
</tr>
<tr>
<td>Introverts are over-stimulated and emotionally exhausted in school.

Teachers are not sure how to adjust instruction for this personality type.</td>
<td>Teachers:<ul><li>Learn the traits of a gifted introvert.</li><li>Make choice central to the educational experience.</li><li>Redefine "participation" in class.</li><li>Reconfigure workspaces to create a quiet zone.</li><li>Allow for a quiet zone at recess (read books, play cards, use sidewalk chalk).</li><li>Create flow between social and reflective activities.</li><li>Don't put children on the spot.</li></ul>Parents:<ul><li>Don't overschedule children.</li><li>Allow time for children to transition between activities.</li><li>Give children some time and space to process what is going on at home.</li><li>Introduce children to new situations and people slowly.</li><li>Help children cultivate their passions.</li><li>Listen carefully to make sure your children feel heard.</li><li>Acknowledge children's strengths and positive attributes.</li></ul></td>
<td><ul><li>Schools' instruction and environments are adjusted to meet the needs of all students.</li></ul>Students:<ul><li>Feel more comfortable in schools.</li><li>Are not exhausted by mid-day.</li><li>Embrace their personality type.</li></ul></td>
</tr>
</table>

Students struggle to make and maintain lasting friendships.	**Parents and teachers:** • Provide opportunities to meet children with similar interests/hobbies, as well as like-minded children or intellectual peers. • Allow friendships with students of different ages. • Practice social skills. • Show sensitivity and help children navigate through difficult experiences with friendships.	**Students:** • Social and emotional skills improve. • Connect with at least one or two children he/she can trust. • Enjoy spending quality time in and out of school with friends.

Chapter 6

Melvin's Story: Gifted with Executive Function Disorder, Spatial Dysgraphia, and Speech Difficulties

Getting to Know My Student

I knew immediately Melvin was going to be fun to work with in my classes. His friendly, outgoing personality attracted other children. Although he suffered from an early speech disorder, his enthusiasm to learn never suffered.

Melvin was a tactile learner. He enjoyed building with any materials he could get his hands on. He often asked, "Can I bring my Legos to school and show you what I am building?" Soon after entering elementary school, Melvin's mother arranged play dates with other boys from his class so they could have endless hours inspiring each other to think creatively.

It was always a joy to hear Melvin talk about his family and the things they enjoyed doing together. He often told his teachers and classmates about his family's travels when we returned from school holidays. Melvin's ability to explain in detail the high points of each trip made one feel he could be a tour guide for the places he visited.

When Melvin started school, he experienced difficulties keeping up with his classmates. He never finished his work, was not ready to follow classroom rules, and had some trouble communicating with his peers. He was then (and still is) a very determined boy. Now in junior high school, Melvin rarely takes no for an answer. He is one of the strongest mathematicians and debaters I have worked with in my classes. I will always remember one time he said, "I never knew I would be so good at arguing points of view in class debates. In elementary school, I had trouble just speaking to my friends."

Parenting Melvin

"He is gifted 24/7"
~Melvin's mother

Unlike many parents of gifted students, Melvin's parents did not describe their son as bright or gifted before he entered school. In their words, he was in the normal range for walking, talking, and reading. However, they did notice that Melvin had adult-type appreciation for things such as classical music, nature, and animals. He also had obsessions with cats and the color yellow. Before first grade testing revealed Melvin was gifted, his parents described their son as "different" and "quirky." They realized these subtle differences might cause their son to stand out once he started school, and they wondered whether school would be a positive or negative experience for him.

During kindergarten and first grade, Melvin's teachers were in frequent contact with his parents. It was during this period that his parents realized that gifted children sometimes don't behave as people would expect. After second grade, Melvin's parents were certain their son was not only smart, but also had some type of learning disability. They saw his handwriting was illegible and he avoided any type of writing activity. Melvin also had trouble completing multistep tasks or projects. They knew his speech was causing issues because Melvin often shared his frustrations about difficulties speaking with classmates. It would become their mission throughout Melvin's education to find the best ways for their son to learn.

Melvin's parents recognized, as do other parents of gifted children, that having an exceptionally talented child was both a delight and a challenge. They fully enjoyed the wonderful things they could do with their young son. Melvin and his parents often read "phenomenal thought -provoking and emotionally intense books" together and enjoyed every minute of that time.

That was the good part. The flip side, however, was that parenting Melvin was often draining. Melvin would cry at the drop of the hat when something upset him, and it would take a long time to calm him. For example, when the family played games such as Monopoly, Melvin would have full scale meltdowns if he lost. The up-and-down swings they experienced at home were tiresome, annoying, and exhausting. In addition, Melvin's mother said it was difficult to arrange playdates at other children's homes because many parents did not feel comfortable handling Melvin's emotions.

When Melvin started school, it was another mixed bag. Melvin's mother had to constantly stay on top of what he needed to succeed in school. The myth that smart kids will be fine without extra support bothered her. Her reality was that Melvin did not need to spend a lot of time reviewing for tests, but he required special accommodations for particular learning challenges such as poor attention/highly distractable and staying organized. Making sure teachers remembered to differentiate for Melvin's strengths as well as his areas of need required daily attentiveness. Too many times, Melvin's mother had to contact a teacher to make sure they had not forgotten the details of her son's Individual Education Plan or IEP. This sometimes-caused teachers to feel that Melvin was receiving more than his fair share of their time.

Parents have many options to choose from when it comes to educating their children, like public school, parochial school, special schools for gifted students, charter schools, and home-schooling. What is most important in making the choice is that the school does not believe that—one size or one method fits all students.

Melvin's parents decided a parochial school was the best fit because they wanted their son to be taught the values of their faith. After Melvin began school, his parents became strong advocates for him, supporting a variety of his needs. They told other parents it was their job to understand any difficulty or concern their child had in school. Parents need to be proactive, asking questions at the first sign of a potential problem.

Melvin's parents noticed a certain type of teacher always brought out the best in their son. Each year they spoke to the principal about teacher traits that would make the biggest impact in Melvin's education. They knew that a teacher who did not rush to judgement and who appreciated every child's differences was important. Melvin was also cautious about teachers who made incorrect statements about the content they were teaching. He did not have a lot of confidence that he could learn from such a teacher. Therefore, Melvin's parents did their best to make sure their son had the right school setting and teachers that enhanced his changes of having a positive educational experience.

In Melvin's gifted classes, he completed many above-grade level assignments that strengthened his creative and critical thinking skills. Although in his regular classroom staying on task could be a problem for Melvin, in his gifted classes he was always fully engaged as he worked on challenging and rigorous assignments. His parents never feared getting a phone call from his teacher telling them he was not working to his full potential. In addition, Melvin told his parents he enjoyed his gifted classes because he could take risks, make mistakes, and learn at his own pace.

In addition to being pleased their son had a place in school where he could develop his strengths and work on social and emotional skills, Melvin's parents were happy to have me on board to support and advocate for their entire family. As a specialist in gifted education, I made sure those who worked directly with Melvin had the most current information about any educational decisions made on his behalf. His parents knew they could find answers to their questions about raising a smart boy by accessing resources provided by the school's gifted education program. Overall, Melvin's family was very thankful for the opportunities their son had in school, even though they sometimes had to advocate strongly for the accommodations he required.

Teaching Melvin

First Grade

Within a few weeks of the beginning of a new school year, as a gifted interventionist, I know that I will be contacted by the teacher who has been assigned their grade level's group of high-potential students. After a brief discussion with the teacher, usually I discover one or more of the following things. A student

- Is not following directions.
- Is not getting classwork done in a timely manner.
- Is overly energetic.
- Is not getting along with peers.
- Has stress or anxiety issues

I wasn't surprised, then, when I heard from a first-grade teacher who had been assigned a small group of smart children, students who were already reading, solving complex math problems, and speaking with advanced vocabularies. She emailed me for help soon after the second week of school because one of the students did not fit the parameters of an extra-smart student.

As previously mentioned, a common misconception about gifted kids is that they breeze through school with no problems, complete schoolwork, organize materials efficiently, and develop friendships easily. This is not always the case. Many gifted children have difficulty with learning and relationships. Melvin's teacher was certain he was bright because he thought differently from his peers, had advanced knowledge in several areas, and his problem-solving ability was exceptional. But he struggled with incomplete work, immaturity, and speech difficulties. A professional assessment completed this year indicated that he seemed to have executive function issues.

Melvin was very small for his age. He seemed to be kind and sensitive. But he had difficulty communicating and listening to others. He wanted to talk only about his own interests. As I watched Melvin participate in various activities, it was clear he was more proficient in some than others. If there were things to manipulate and observe, he was on board. He also could focus for long periods if the lesson included advanced math problems or complicated puzzles.

However, Melvin was not interested in finishing any task that involved writing. After many observations, I concluded that Melvin could be twice exceptional.

At the first parent-teacher conference, both teacher and parents were apprehensive because Melvin was not working at grade level in all areas. His mother said that he was unhappy about going to school, and she saw that many of the papers in his take-home folder were incomplete. She was confused because she knew her son grasped concepts quickly and displayed knowledge well beyond that of an average six-year-old. The teacher pointed out that Melvin's classmates were beginning to ignore him because he had difficulty with his speech, and he seemed immature. She said Melvin lacked general understanding of things such as personal boundaries, following simple directions, and taking turns. The adults agreed that an intervention plan with small, achievable goals was essential.

Melvin's teacher and parents communicated often about his progress. His mother expressed that she and her husband were considering moving their son to another school. But after giving it more thought, they realized they should give Melvin adequate time to reach his goals. His speech was improving with the help of a speech pathologist, and he was making small gains both socially and emotionally.

The school staff hoped that his parents would decide he was in the best place for elementary school. In addition to receiving support for specific academic, social, and speech goals, Melvin was identified as gifted in late spring by a first-grade ability test administered at the school.

When his parents were given this information, they were surprised. They knew their son was smart, but the term *gifted* was new to them. Like many people, these parents needed to understand that giftedness in children does not always look like what most people expect. During the last week of school, I contacted Melvin's parents and told them he would receive gifted services (noticeable differences in both curriculum and instructional materials compared to the general education curriculum) in second grade. I also wanted them to know they would receive consultative services to learn how to advocate for their son. I had no doubt that with a knowledgeable team of teachers, a gifted specialist, and caring parents, Melvin would continue making progress and reach his fullest potential.

Second Grade

When first grade ended, Melvin's parents were still grappling with the idea that a gifted boy could experience learning difficulties. Although the second-grade teacher felt she was ready to work with Melvin after our initial conversation, she observed that he was often overwhelmed by simple tasks. For example, students were told to put their names and dates on every paper and to place all finished work in designated baskets in the classroom. In addition, students kept textbooks and workbooks and other supplies in their desks. For most students, this would not be a big deal, but for Melvin, it was. In her correspondence to me, the teacher stated, "I cannot understand how a gifted boy needs so much repetition for basic organizational skills." This told me that Melvin's teacher did not understand that smart kids can also have learning disabilities, and it was necessary for me to intervene and explain twice-exceptionality.

The partnership between parents and teacher continued and things improved. Melvin's mother recognized that her son was doing better at completing assignments this year, with fewer incomplete papers. Nonetheless, all the adults agreed that Melvin needed continued help with organizational skills and following directions.

Organization Help

Even before Melvin was officially diagnosed with Executive Function Disorder (EFD), his teacher believed that children should have an important stake in their own education. She spoke with him about the importance of organization in school, at home, and in life, and it was at this point that she made an important decision. She asked Melvin to suggest ways he might organize his work more effectively. If gifted children are given the opportunity, they sometimes think deeply and find solutions to their own problems. Melvin's teacher worked to address his giftedness as well as his disability.

Melvin felt empowered by his teacher's trust. He looked around the room and noticed that the class library was color-coded. His teacher put stickers on the books according to their reading levels so students did not waste time searching for an appropriate book. He thought color-coding might work for his desk.

Melvin suggested to his teacher that his textbooks should have green covers and the workbooks should have yellow covers labeled with their subject titles in large black letters. He also thought he should put his textbooks on the left side of his desk and the workbooks on the right. This method of organizing books became popular with his classmates, too, and some of them requested their books be color-coded as well.

The teacher discovered that Melvin didn't always know where he should put his work when he finished it. He sometimes simply jammed it into his desk, which meant that his work was often marked as incomplete. His teacher then clearly labeled the baskets in the room and color-coded each one. The students knew that if they got their work turned in on time, they would receive immediate feedback from their teacher.

At home, Melvin's mother supported her son with organization guidance. She wanted him to put away his clothes, toys, and school things instead of scattering them around his bedroom. When Melvin told his mother he had helped design a plan to find the books and materials he needed in class, she asked him if he would like to do something similar at home. Melvin excitedly agreed that by color-coding drawers in his dresser and labeling shelves in his room, he could do a better job keeping things in their place. Goals common to both school and home made it easier for Melvin to find success. He ceased making excuses again for losing things or being unprepared to learn. Because he played a big part in developing his own goals, he gave his personal best each day. It wasn't long before both Melvin's teacher and parents observed measurable progress at home and school.

After helping Melvin become better organized, his teacher spoke with him about a listening goal. She wanted him (and his classmates) to understand the difference between *hearing* and *listening*. She told Melvin he was missing important directions in class because he was passively listening or just hearing "noise" when people spoke. She began to use the phrase "eyes on the speaker" every time she or a classmate needed to tell the class something. When the children heard this phrase, they were directed to turn their body toward the speaker and look the person directly in the eye. To reinforce organization and listening skills, the teacher placed a laminated card with simple reminders on each student's desk.

I will have my materials ready to learn. 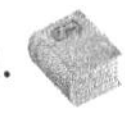

I will put finished work in the proper place. 

I will look at the speaker. 

Executive Function Disorder

Although Melvin had made progress in many areas of second grade, his parents felt he still showed signs of being out of sync with his peers. With a referral from the parent of another gifted child, they met with a psychologist who worked with high-potential children. After several visits, Melvin was diagnosed with Executive Function Disorder (EFD), which causes a student to have trouble with organization and task completion.

Note: Children with EFD can struggle to organize materials, regulate emotions, set schedules, and stick to tasks. They often misplace papers, reports, and other school materials.[95]

With this diagnosis, a more definitive plan could be put into place for teachers and parents to help support Melvin with the execution of daily tasks at school and home. As the end of the second grade neared, it was important to plan for increased success in third grade. With the support of caring parents, who said they were happy they had not changed schools after first grade, I knew we could continue to smooth the bumpy road for Melvin, who was showing gains academically, socially, and emotionally.

Third Grade

Before the first day of third grade, I met with Melvin's new teacher. She had been assigned the group of gifted students and was eager to learn about them. In our discussion, I focused on Melvin but explained that there was no clear-cut profile of a twice-exceptional student.

A child can be gifted and at the same time have dyslexia, visual or auditory processing problems, obsessive-compulsive disorder, or other disabilities that interfere with the student's ability to learn effectively in a traditional environment. By helping Melvin's teacher understand he was gifted but struggled with executive function disorder, we could prevent him from backsliding in third grade.

We also discussed that the physical act of writing was labor-intensive for Melvin, and if he was pressed to finish something on a deadline, he became quite stressed, and his work was often messy and difficult to read.

Dysgraphia

Dysgraphia is a neurological disorder characterized by writing disabilities. In children, the disorder generally emerges when they are first introduced to writing. They make inappropriately sized and spaced letters, or write wrong or misspelled words, despite thorough instruction.[96]

Melvin had worked with an occupational therapist over the summer who diagnosed him with spatial dysgraphia, a disorder affecting written expression. Unlike dyslexia, which is difficulty with reading, a child with dysgraphia may read well but not be able to put ideas down on paper. The student's work looks sloppy, as if he or she isn't trying very hard. But the student may be making a tremendous effort, whether or not the results show that. The child simply has a much harder time writing than his peers do.

To overcome Melvin's problems with writing, the therapist utilized multisensory techniques, and his teacher allowed handwriting warm-ups and writing breaks to fight fatigue. The teacher also used outlines and graphic organizers to break projects into shorter tasks. Melvin also began intensive instruction in keyboarding.

Creative writing activities, such as pen pals, a class post office, or journaling, are activities all teachers should explore with their students; but for children like Melvin such strategies are essential. If students recognize writing as merely a way to fill out worksheets or responses to questions, they will never experience the enjoyment of writing for other purposes. Melvin's teacher provided writing and drawing time in her classroom, and she asked the children to take their journals home and write about anything of interest to them.

By the end of the first quarter of school, Melvin's teacher handed me his journal. As I read the numerous stories on the pages, I was pleasantly surprised: Melvin's writing was neat, and his spelling was commendable. His teacher told me the dramatic improvement was in part because she had reduced the amount of copying her students were required to do. Instead, she focused on the more creative aspects of writing, not just for Melvin, but for all her students. In fact, his accommodations, from color-coding, to "eyes on the speaker," to a new style of teaching writing, benefited all the children.

Single-Subject Acceleration

From the time Melvin entered school, his parents watched his academic, social, and emotional growth carefully, and if any areas concerned them, they did not hesitate to ask questions. After observing Melvin excel at math all year, they broached the idea of single-subject acceleration. Melvin's mother knew his teacher had been differentiating for her son in math since the second semester of school, and he always made A's. The teacher described Melvin's ability to solve advanced math problems as "mind boggling."

When additional data had been collected (including classroom math grades, grade level assessments, and teacher/parent questionnaires about the student's math ability), it appeared that subject acceleration was a definite possibility. Melvin's parents took him back to the clinic that had identified his executive function disorder and requested both an ability test and a math achievement test. Melvin's math score fell into the superior range, and his new ability score was 153, remarkably high. As a result, the Intervention Assistance Team deemed him an excellent candidate for math acceleration.

Note: Melvin was not recommended for whole-grade acceleration because his level of academic development varied from subject to subject. He struggled in language arts and often required extra help to master grade level standards in this subject. Also, Melvin was not socially or emotionally ready to skip an entire grade level.

Fourth Grade

Fourth grade was the first time Melvin would transition between four different teachers for his classes, which could be a challenge to his executive planning and organizational skills. In addition to changing classes, he would also be taking fifth-grade math. But with high expectations and the proper support, his teachers felt confident he would be successful.

After a few weeks, Melvin's team of teachers and I met to discuss his progress with fourth-grade responsibilities. It was important to make sure we were all following the same road map to help Melvin reach fourth grade goals. If one teacher caused a detour by inadvertently not supporting his special needs, the effects could be detrimental to his overall progress. We all agreed he was doing well and did not appear to be stressed. He also seemed to be excited that he was exploring fifth-grade math.

Nonetheless, when one teacher mentioned that Melvin often needed to have directions repeated several times, we were concerned some multistep assignments might be problematic for him. The team felt it might be helpful to assign Melvin a "study buddy" for each class. These helpers could remind him of any instructions he missed to help avoid a potential melt-down. Although most upper elementary children are expected to manage multiple classes, assignments, and deadlines, we realized that Melvin needed this assistance until he felt more confident.

During this year, Melvin continued to participate in his school's gifted program. It was clear he felt more relaxed in these classes because the schedule to finish work was more flexible. Also, as a result of continuing speech therapy, Melvin enjoyed talking more about his interests, and it seemed his peers liked listening to him as well. This significantly increased his self-esteem.

The students in his gifted classes began to learn more about common gifted characteristics, such as perfectionism and heightened intensity, and how some of these qualities can be problematic. I made it a point to teach the students the meaning of twice-exceptional. Like most students, they were surprised to discover that some gifted people can also have a learning disability. My goal for the students was to make sure they understood that when an individual has special needs, it is important to embrace the differences rather than make negative judgements. When Melvin heard this, he began to talk openly about being 2e, and his need for extra assistance with his schoolwork. When he spoke to others in this way, I knew a significant roadblock on Melvin's trip had been removed.

Here is a note from Melvin's Fourth Grade Teacher:

> *I knew Melvin had some concerns with school when he began fourth grade. He needed extra help with organizational skills, and he seemed a bit immature compared to his peers. I noticed he would say things in class that other kids did not understand. Or if he told a joke, no one laughed but me. It appeared his feelings got hurt easily when this happened. But he did have one close friend he enjoyed at school. Weekend playdates were also arranged for the two boys. I would overhear them talk about video games and other fun things they did together. This relationship helped a lot because in general Melvin had trouble making friends.*
>
> *By the end of fourth grade, I could tell Melvin had grown a lot, particularly socially and emotionally. He had taken responsibility for his own learning by staying on top of what he needed for his classes, and he was prepared for tests. The goals he achieved made him feel better about himself. Finally, I was happy to hear him talk about the chance to work with sixth grade pre-algebra students in the next year. I think the experience of subject acceleration in math will continue to propel Melvin toward his fullest potential.*

Melvin's Reflections:

> *When I first heard that I was identified as gifted in first grade, I thought I was going to get a gift! Now I understand it means I learn differently and need more challenges in school. Sometimes school is very easy for me in subjects like science, social studies, and math. When I was in first grade, I thought my science lessons were for kindergarten because they were so*

> *easy. I would say my weakness in school is writing because I feel I am terrible at it.*
>
> *My personal strength is my sense of humor. I also feel I have a few close friendships. They are people who understand how my brain works because their brain works in the same way. My personal weakness is sports. They are hard for me. When kids pick teams, I am the last one chosen. And when the game finally starts, sometimes other kids kick me out. That hurts my feelings.*
>
> *I enjoy several hobbies. They include reading, building with Legos, talking with my friends, and playing video games. When read, I enjoy scary stories, mythology, and nonfiction books. When I build with Legos, it sometimes takes me several days to finish my designs. I also enjoy playing with my sister and our pet cat.*
>
> *As a gifted boy, I know I have special people who support me. When I think about the kind of teachers I enjoy, I think of those who make me feel challenged. They also understand me and don't judge me because I'm different. I also like teachers I can have interesting conversations with at school.*
>
> *At home, my mom is supporting by watching educational shows with me and helping me find books at the library I might enjoy. She accepts me for who I am. My dad supports me by sharing my interests in history and social studies. Although I don't play sports very much, I enjoy watching college football games with my dad. Finally, my gifted classes support me because we work on more difficult assignments. I like having time to work with other smart kids like me too. My gifted class and math class are my favorite parts of school.*

Melvin's story is a good one to point out that we should never make judgements about 2e children. Too many adults don't consider acceleration a good move for gifted children, particularly one that has a learning disability. However, Melvin and others like him can thrive in school if their thirst is quenched in the subject they excel at.

Table 6.1. Road Trip Assistance for Students like Melvin

Roadblock	RoadMap	Destination
Students are not motivated to complete class assignments.	**Teachers:** • Determine reasons for incomplete work. • Make sure students understand purpose/ benefits of assignments. • Set small realistic/ achievable goals with student input. • Provide positive redirection. • Create positive classroom environment by maintaining open and responsive attitude.	**Students:** • Overcome discouragement. • Gain confidence as goals are achieved. • Seek support from teacher and family. • Establish routine to cultivate discipline.
Students are immature compared to peers.	**Teachers and parents:** • Assign non-academic tasks to build success. • Provide opportunities to work/play in small groups with structured activities. • Understand individuals vary in their rate of development. • Be aware of overprotection, which may cause children to behave in immature ways. • Monitor for bullies who may single out immature, anxious classmates.	**Students:** • Receive acknowledgment for small accomplishments. • Improve social and relationship skills. • Build self-esteem and confidence.

Students have poor spatial relationships with peers.	**Teachers and parents:** • Role-play appropriate ways to stand near friends and family. • Play games to help develop spatial awareness (Legos, construction toys, tangrams, other spatial puzzles. • Supply children with directions including spatial language (behind, next to, beside). • Encourage children to use gestures when solving spatial problems.	**Students:** • Develop spatial skills. • Use spatial language with teachers, classmates, and family members. • Have an increased awareness of people's personal space. • Improve relationships with classmates.
Students are diagnosed with dysgraphia.	**Teachers and parents:** • Add occupational therapists to the team of professionals who support students' needs. • Provide remediation in letter form and fluency to younger children. • Instruct students in how to use preorganization strategies (graphic organizers) when writing paragraphs. • Instruct in word processing skills. • Eliminate copying tasks. • Provide copies of class notes. • Allow extra time to write. • Do not penalize for poor spelling or neatness on first drafts. • Offer students alternative ways to express what they have learned (debates, graphs, PowerPoints).	**Students:** • Use warm-up exercises before writing. • Gain strength in hands. • Learn organizational strategies to use when writing paragraphs. • Use word processing programs with ease. • Feel more successful in writing.

Students are diagnosed with executive function disorder.	**Teachers and parents:** • Color code and clearly label baskets, trays, shelves, and other receptacles for items, both at school and at home. • Instruct students in how to use and maintain a daily schedule, planner, or calendar, with apps such as *Google Calendar* or *ToDoist*. • Teach self-regulation skills by playing card and board games and using apps such as *30/30* or *InClass* (for older students). • Provide children with positive feedback for accomplishments.	**Students:** • Locate materials easily. • Put items in their proper places. • Improve time-on-task. • Improve self-regulation skills (behaviors, emotions, thoughts). • Give their personal best each day to stay organized.
Students exhibit speech deficiencies that affect peer relationships and self-esteem.	**Teachers and parents:** • Include speech therapists as part of students' diagnostic teams. • Determine type of speech disorder: articulation, fluency, resonance. • Implement language intervention activities and articulation therapies. • Help students to understand that good oral communication is as important as clear written communication. • Be patient and understanding with children.	**Students:** • Practice therapists' stimulation activities. • Achieve goals to articulate sounds correctly and produce clear language. • Become more comfortable speaking with others. • Build confidence and self-esteem.

Students work well above same-age peers in one or more subject areas such as math, reading, language arts, science, social studies.	**Teachers:** • Differentiate strength areas by changing: ***pace*** (curriculum compacting, tiered assignments in content, and/or product), ***content*** (mini-lessons, different resources, independent studies and ***product*** (choice boards, menus, technology products such as websites/podcasts).[97] • Consider single-subject acceleration so students can work at higher grade levels to access appropriate learning opportunities.	**Students:** • Enjoy challenging work with true peers. • Develop perseverance through higher-level work assignments. • Move at an appropriate pace and continue to grow academically in areas of strength. • Stay motivated about school.

Chapter 7
Jake's Story
Highly Gifted with a Language Learning Disability

Getting to Know My Student

Engaging, passionate, and strong-minded are all adjectives that come to mind when I think of Jake. From the time he was a young boy, his eyes shined brightly with excitement when he was learning something new. Though he often experienced educational roadblocks, he stood firm and communicated persuasively (despite his language learning disability) his need to succeed to those who could sometimes throw roadblocks in his path.

Jake's body language always told the story of his work to survive in school. If he shrugged his shoulders, rolled his eyes, or needed time to vent about problems, teachers and friends knew it was not a good day for Jake. But if he came bouncing down the hallway with a smile asking everyone dozens of questions, it was evident Jake was having an exhilarating day. Like so many gifted children, he was intense in whatever he felt or did.

Strong personal goals and a sensitive ear to others' struggles set Jack apart from his classmates. If he thought something was unfair, like how his high school peers' GPAs were miscalculated or when the school district removed Wikipedia from its schools' technology labs, Jake would step forward to talk with the adults in charge. He understood the decisions made by a few affected many.

One of Jake's respected high school teachers summed it up best when he said, "His candor, drive, and motivated personality often caught others off guard. The desire to correct injustice and fight for the underdog drove Jake to ask tough questions and not be afraid of the reactions he might get. At all times, he advocated for his own learning and focused clearly on what needed to be done."

Parenting Jake

"It's not easy. It's not easy at all raising a gifted child."

~Jake's mother

From a very young age, Jake was a hands-on child who needed to be constantly stimulated in his environment. His family read and spoke with him often, and when he got a little older, they took him to restaurants, car shows, the beach, and on an occasional airplane trip. Even with all these extra stimuli in his life, there were times Jake's mother thought her son was unhappy because she felt he still had not been given enough attention. She described her son's intensity as all-consuming.

When she reflected on the amazing gift she had been given having such a bright child, her first thoughts were that it would be easy to raise her son. In reality, it was not. Sometimes she felt Jake's giftedness was similar to children with disabilities. He could not sit still and remember his manners. Even at birthday parties his family noticed all the other children playing together doing age-appropriate things. Jake, however, was more interested in speaking with the adults and exploring the things that came in the gift bags. Each day presented its own set of dilemmas to figure out.

When Jake turned three, his family knew he was ready for pre-school, and they looked for a school that would allow Jake the freedom to learn and grow at this own pace. His mother was happy to find a Montessori school near their home. It was known for its creative teachers who engaged their students with numerous hands-on activities.

Although Jake's first school provided the flexibility he required to make progress, he showed early signs of frustration when he felt he was being micromanaged at home. He appreciated insight and help from his family, but always wanted to be independent and in control. These first experiences with Jake's development let his mother know that once her son entered public school with its rules, assignments with deadlines and other regulations, there might be some problems. She prepared herself for the many interesting issues that would arise in the process of educating a very smart boy.

Jake's mom knew her experience raising her son was different from most families. She always appreciated the times when she learned with him. When Jake showed signs of early independence and learning on his own terms, she thought she would not have to guide her child every step of the way through school.

However, the tide turned as Jake entered public school. She immediately noticed that her parenting style would have to change by the time her son entered fourth grade. There were power struggles at every turn because Jake questioned everything and openly refused to be controlled. He was very strong-willed.

In addition to numerous confrontations with her son, Jake's mother often found herself on an uneven playing field when speaking about her son to other people. Many families and friends knew how smart he was and how well he did in school, so it was not uncommon for other parents to ask Jake's mother for advice about how to handle certain concerns they experienced with their children. Some of the more popular questions she was asked were "How do you get your child to complete his homework without spending hours on it each night?" and "How does your child study to get such good grades?" She did her best not to offend anyone who asked these questions, but the reality of her situation was far different from talking about a child's not finishing his homework or getting good grades on a report card. She had no one to listen to her concerns about parenting Jake. If she attempted to discuss her issues, others would say she was complaining about raising a smart kid-and that was a good problem to have!

In addition, if she told someone her son won a contest or advanced to a state level academic competition, others became jealous and felt she was bragging. Therefore, Jake's mother never got to revel in her son's accomplishments the way other parents did. "Most people just don't get it. They say you are so lucky your child makes straight A's.

Instead of enduring the challenge of other parents who don't understand the real difficulties, the parent of a gifted child could respond: 1) You are so lucky your child can hit a ball. 2) You are so lucky the first parenting manual you tried worked. 3) You are so lucky you can spell words to your spouse and expect that your two-year old won't understand. 4) You are so lucky your child hasn't been literally bored to tears in their classroom. 5) You are so lucky your teachers are always happy to see your child in the classroom."[98]

Teaching Jake

Kindergarten

Jake's kindergarten teacher recalled that her new student made a strong first impression. He arrived at school in khaki pants, a dress shirt with a little tie, and dress shoes. She felt he was dressed for success. From the beginning, she was delighted and amazed with his exceptional verbal skills. At five, Jake could carry on extended conversations related to just about any topic. She observed he often seemed more comfortable speaking with adults rather than peers and said he was very adept at handling the give and take of conversations.

As kindergarten progressed, Jake showed other signs that he was a very smart boy. He understood and enjoyed sarcasm and had a wonderful sense of humor. He sometimes rolled his eyes when he saw or heard things peers said that did not make sense to him. He grasped concepts quickly.

Despite his obvious talents, Jake was his own harshest critic and judge. A true perfectionist, he expected to do his best work one hundred percent of the time. When he did not meet a self-imposed benchmark, he would often get quiet and sometimes cry. This behavior is typical of asynchronous gifted children (exceptional talent out of 'synch' with normal behavior parameters) who can see the result they want to achieve but might not yet have the skills to carry it out, and who suffer inordinately when they fail.

Socially, Jake enjoyed a wide variety of activities in kindergarten, including learning centers, puzzles, Legos, and blocks. He always waited for his turn and shared with his classmates; Jake's teacher described him as respectful and polite with everyone. He liked to follow the rules, and he did not know what to make of children who did not. When Jake tried to have extended verbal dialogue with a peer about a rule, the other children would frequently ignore his efforts, and his teacher would have to intervene. Overall, Jake was an extrovert who enjoyed people and learning all he could, regardless of his young age; but sometimes others saw him as strong-willed and somewhat bossy.

First Grade

When it was time for Jake to move to first grade, his parents discovered that the school their son attended offered a multiage program for elementary students. If desired, they could select for their son a classroom setting consisting of both first and second grade children. This type of learning environment included individual student goals written by the teacher, parents, and child, and the opportunity to work with the same teacher for two years. Jake's family liked the idea their son would not be limited by a specific grade-level curriculum based on age. If a child showed mastery of a first-grade skill, he was immediately allowed to progress to the second-grade level. Conversely, if a child required more time to master a concept, he could work on it without fear of judgement by anyone. Jake also liked the idea of being with one teacher for two years.

The multi-age classroom was a perfect fit for Jake. His teacher noticed immediately that he worked above grade level in math, science, and communication skills, but that he lagged in reading and writing. She worked with him in small groups to improve his reading skills and provided opportunities for him to excel in math and use his communication skills.

During the summer, after nine months in the multiage classroom, Jake's family moved, which required him to attend another elementary school in the same district. He could not continue working with his multiage classmates. But at his new school there was an amazing second-grade teacher who had been a multiage teacher before, and who practiced many of the strategies he had experienced in first grade. She excelled at helping her students set individual learning goals, think critically and creatively, and evaluate their own work. Jake was not happy to move and leave his friends behind, but his parents counseled him to have an open mind about all the possibilities at the new school. It was good advice. Second grade was going to offer life-long changes for Jake, and all of it was good.

Second Grade

As I was walking down the second-grade hallway at one of the three schools I served, a teacher asked to speak with me about a student who had transferred from another school in our district. She described him as inquisitive and like a sponge because he soaked up any new knowledge taught in class. She also mentioned he preferred speaking with her instead of his peers and seemed older than his chronological age. I knew immediately she was talking about Jake.

Jake's teacher and I met often to discuss her observations of him. One day, she shared a particularly interesting story. She had assigned pairs of students in her class the task of researching a famous American. Students were encouraged to locate additional information at home and bring it to class as well.

Jake was initially very excited about his research, and the very next day brought several resources to school to show his teacher. When he found out his partner had done nothing in preparation for the project, his excitement diminished. Jake's mother contacted his teacher and discussed her son's unhappiness; she asked if he could work by himself on the project. Fortunately, Jake's teacher was flexible about how her students learned. Working independently, Jake presented one of the best research projects his second-grade teacher had ever seen. That wouldn't have happened had the teacher not allowed a relaxation of her rules. It was better that she inspired, stimulated, and motivated him to use his mind to the fullest.[99]

In addition to setting the right classroom climate, where students know they are respected and valued for their uniqueness, great teachers—like Jake's—support the variety of different needs exhibited by their students. Jake's teacher saw that he was strong verbally, but poor at writing. He did not care about perfecting the grammar, mechanics, and spelling of his written work at this level of his education. Therefore, she encouraged him with strength-based instruction. (Teachers utilize the student's strengths to support their areas of need.) He was allowed to record stories and reports on a tape recorder that otherwise would have required lots of writing. Then a scribe typed a copy for Jake and his teacher to discuss. By making this simple adjustment, Jake's weaknesses were minimized, and his strengths maximized.

In addition to writing concerns, Jake was not reading at grade level. His teacher felt he would benefit from more focused instruction with a reading specialist. He needed help on fluency, decoding skills, and writing. Jake's teacher was certain that his ability to learn quickly would allow him to catch up with remediation. But I was concerned that Jake might have a language-based learning disability because of problems with age-appropriate reading, spelling, and writing.[100] Jake could demonstrate solid knowledge in a class discussion and speak as though he was much older than his age, but he could not read or write at grade level.

Language Learning Disability

Note: "The most commonly used approach in diagnosing learning disabilities is to compare some measures of the person's ability or potential with other measures that reflect that person's achievement. If the achievement is falling significantly below what would be expected, based on the estimate of ability, a learning disability is suspected, unless there are other factors that could more easily account for the discrepancy."[101]

Jake's second grade teacher referred him to the school's Intervention Team to discuss a possible language-based learning disability. "Language based learning disability (LBLD) refers to a spectrum of difficulties related to the understanding and use of spoken and written language. It can manifest as a wide variety of language difficulties with different levels of severity. One student may have difficulty sounding out words for reading or spelling but have no difficulty with oral expression or listening comprehension."[102] (This described Jake.) After the school psychologist completed a battery of assessments, Jake was indeed diagnosed with a language-based learning disability. Although some students with LBLD experience minor interferences that may be addressed in class, some students may need specialized, individualized attention throughout their school day in order to develop fluent language skills. Jake worked with a reading specialist several times a week.

During the spring, the CogAT (Cognitive Abilities Test) was administered to all second graders. This test would measure reasoning and the problem-solving skills most directly related to academic success. The results would provide valuable information for guidance with lesson planning in the regular classroom, and identification for gifted programs. Jake's teacher and I both felt he was gifted, but we were concerned a test administered to a whole group might not reveal true results for a student who struggled with certain aspects of learning. An individual test, rather than a group test, would be better.[103] Our instinct was confirmed when the test data came back, and Jake was *not* identified as gifted despite our many observations indicating otherwise. We could not determine what factors, such as his language disability or classroom environment, affected his results.

However, Jake's case was a good one to take to the administration to show why it is important to have a multifaceted identification process that includes information from a variety of sources such as family, teachers, outside experts, and those who work with the student away from school like scout leaders, music teachers, and sport coaches. Student observations, performances, products/portfolios, and interviews are equally important. *No single assessment method or score should ever be relied upon for making such high-stakes decisions.* Nonetheless, intelligence tests can still yield useful information when used as part of a comprehensive, multifaceted procedure.[104]

Third Grade

Jake seemed eager to begin third grade, hoping he would learn many new things. He continued to wear the "dress-for-success" clothes he liked: khaki pants, dress shoes, and button-down shirts. It didn't bother him that the other boys were wearing jeans, t-shirts, and athletic shoes.

From the first couple weeks of school, Jake's teacher noticed he had some difficulty focusing on class instruction. She moved his desk to separate him from others, assuming this would help his focus. She wondered if Jake had ADHD, however his first- and second-grade teachers never mentioned this as a concern. At first glance, the lists of characteristic behaviors for ADHD look similar to the characteristics that indicate giftedness. The student may fidget, have difficulty maintaining eye contact, shift from side to side while speaking, be forgetful, daydream, be careless with work, indicate a lack of interest in details, and be very stubborn.[105] However, these same behaviors can arise in a gifted child without ADHD due to educational misplacement when academic needs are not met.

I felt it was important for Jake's academic needs to be met this year so that he would not become frustrated and lose interest in school. Although I was not working with Jake in our school's gifted program, I met with his teacher to discuss the extensive observations made of him during the previous year. One of my hopes was that the successful instructional strategies and methods his second-grade teacher had used would be used for Jake in third grade.

I explained that Jake's high energy and constant need to ask questions were not a sign of ADHD, but part of a bigger picture. I wanted Jake's third-grade teacher to know I felt he was a high potential student despite working below grade level in some areas such as writing. It was crucial to strike a balance between challenging Jake's areas of strength and developing his areas of weakness.

One day, as I was preparing information about Jake for an intervention team meeting, the principal contacted me about a situation. She told me Jake and another boy had been brought in from recess because of an altercation, more verbal than physical. When the boys were sharing their sides of the story, the principal was immediately taken by the eloquence of Jake's speech. The way he explained the details of the recess event made her feel she was speaking with a much older student.

Because Jake had transferred in for second grade, the principal was not as familiar with him as she was with other students. She inquired if I served him in the gifted program. I explained Jake did not qualify according to the school's whole-group testing administered in second grade. At that moment, she made the request for the school psychologist to administer an individual ability test because, like me, she had no doubt Jake was very smart.

No one would have ever guessed a recess altercation would have helped identify a young boy. But when Jake's individual ability test was scored, he was in the exceptionally gifted range. He immediately was offered 'pull-out services' (individualized attention outside of the regular classroom), working with other identified third graders on projects that challenged him in many ways. His ADHD-like behaviors were greatly reduced. Jake's family was also excited to know their son would have a specialist for gifted students to advocate for him, someone to watch over his educational needs as he progressed through school. It was clear that Jake had been ill-served by the school's decision about giftedness being based on only one test.

In third grade, Jake said that the only place he truly felt like he fit in school was in his gifted classes. He waited eagerly for Tuesdays and Thursdays when his gifted classes met. Jake would watch the door of his regular classroom for me to arrive and escort his group to my classroom. He was like a horse at the Kentucky Derby waiting for the gate to be opened so he could run as fast as possible. Jake's time with like peers and a teacher who understood his differences were necessary for survival. On several occasions, Jake asked if he could stay in my class longer because he was not eager to return to his regular third-grade room. He explained it did not fit him academically or socially. When I heard this, it was a challenge to explain why he had to return.

It occurred to me Jake wanted to avoid his regular classroom work because he deemed most of it unimportant: he needed to know up front the significance of any given assignment. He also wanted to show what he knew, being disinclined to do work he felt he had already mastered. Unfortunately, his teacher taught to the whole group instead of differentiating for those who could move ahead. This became a problem for Jake because he had to feel that his time was not being wasted. "Kids don't read Piaget, but they know instinctively that there should be a difference between what is already in their heads and what is being presented in class. They may not have the maturity to carry out the suggestions they make, but that is what the parents and teachers are for: to provide structure, discipline, and loving guidance."[106]

Since first grade, Jake's ability to express himself in written form never matched his advanced speaking ability. Third grade was no different. His teacher tried to help him form complete thoughts in his written work because anyone who read his papers would never have a clear picture of his ability.

The gap between oral and written skills became the focus for Jake and his teachers. It was decided he must learn how to type on a computer keyboard. Many gifted students' minds work faster than their writing hands. Working on a computer can help get thoughts down so they can be easily edited later. Jake understood that it was imperative he learn to type his work, or he would fail language arts. He worked with other gifted students in my classes using self-paced keyboarding programs that allow each child to set personal goals for speed and accuracy once they have mastered finger placement. Jake was excited about the opportunity because he thought he could learn this new skill quickly.

However, learning to keyboard did not come easily for any of the students. The first lessons were difficult for Jake. Although he knew it would help him throughout his life, he did not like feeling uncomfortable. What made matters worse was that the keyboarding program did not allow students to correct their mistakes, and this deficiency almost sent Jake over the edge. In spite of his feelings, he challenged himself each week to succeed at keyboarding goals. As he typed written assignments, he realized he no longer had to take short cuts with his thoughts. He loved that he could move quickly and clean up the writing at a later date. Learning this skill became life-changing for Jake.

Fourth Grade

It is common for teachers to meet at the end of a school year to discuss class placement for the coming year. Since they know the students well, they group them by several factors and the lists are submitted to the principal for review. This year, Jake's school had a new principal, and after the lists were completed, she decided she would allow her teachers to select their students for the coming year. She failed to determine students' needs or which teacher might be best suited for specific groups. She assumed each teacher would select a class based on their own ability to work with the students they chose. This decision set in motion a series of unfortunate events.

In addition to the new principal, the school district had hired an additional fourth-grade teacher for Jake's school. She was a first-year teacher excited to work with an experienced team. But she was not hired until the school year had almost begun, so she did not know the students and had no say about which group of students she would teach. Her grade-level team decided for her and assigned her a class with the cluster of gifted students.

When I arrived at school to begin my year, I was extremely disappointed to discover this news. In the process of class selection, leaving the inexperienced teacher to work with high-potential students reminded me of children picking members for a softball team. Remember the kids who are standing last because no one wants to have them on their team? It seemed to me that the gifted cluster was disregarded, tossed to the new teacher because they were misunderstood.

One of the repercussions of this thoughtless decision was that the new teacher did not have the appropriate time to plan for her fourth grade. Because she was hired late, she was not offered a chance to speak with her team about the types of children she would be working with. I knew I had my work cut out for me, but I was excited about the opportunity to work with a new young teacher. Nonetheless, before I began planning for the year, I met with the fourth-grade team leader and the principal to express my grave concerns.

I told them I felt a very poor educational decision had been made and the philosophy "do no harm" had been thrown out the window when the cluster group of smart kids was placed with an inexperienced teacher. It was clear that the entire staff needed to learn more about the truths of working with gifted children. After meeting with the fourth-grade team, I was hopeful that things would get better, but I also knew this school year was going to be "under construction" for quite a while.

Jake's year began like third grade. He started school hoping he would learn new things, use his strengths during class projects, and perhaps make a friend or two. But within a couple of weeks, his enthusiasm turned to disappointment. He had not made connections with any of his classmates, and he felt his teacher was uncomfortable around him. When I met with Jake during our first gifted class, I could tell that he was bored and frustrated in his regular class. He wanted to move more quickly through the curriculum and talk a lot about his interests with others, but he was not allowed to do either. On one occasion, Jake got into an argument with his teacher in front of others because he felt she didn't understand him at all. The noise level rose to the point the team leader across the hall came over and spoke to Jake about the situation.

Although I worked with Jake's teacher on differentiated units of study for the high-potential students in the class, it also was important to help Jake find ways to express himself. He required stimulating conversations and occasions to express his opinions. I knew if his strong verbal skills were not given an outlet, he would likely have more altercations with his teacher that would only deepen his dislike for school. In their book *Cradles of Eminence*, Victor and Mildred Goertzel write about the childhoods of famous men and women, like Winston Churchill and Pearl Buck, who were highly verbal as children. From their research, the authors concluded, "These burgeoning, exploding, highly verbal boys and girls were undoubtedly problems in their classrooms. They were too eager to get at the truth of things to be satisfied with what they were told."[107]

Fortunately, I remembered each elementary school in the district had a student council, which allowed interested children to participate in group projects to help others. Often these students spoke to the school in assemblies about things such as recycling, helping the disadvantaged, and promoting school fundraisers. This opportunity was perfect for Jake because he could incorporate his strengths and interests while being a member of an active group in the school. His mother and I encouraged him to get involved.

Once he was selected to participate on the student council, Jake began to enjoy school again. It was a lifeline thrown to him when he was starting to drown. Gifted children often learn early that being precocious and highly verbal can be annoying to some teachers, so they must figure out how to fit in and develop who they are over time.[108] If it had not been for the student council, I believe it would have been difficult for Jake to avoid becoming a discipline problem.

During a couple of in-depth conversations, Jake told me he wanted to be an attorney. At about this time, he started wearing men's ties to school with his dress shirts because his grandfather had taught him to tie a Windsor knot. He seemed very proud to show off his new skill by wearing a variety of neckties to school.

I remembered hearing Jake say that dressing this way made him feel more confident. I also remembered his kindergarten teacher saying that when Jake dressed up for school, she felt he was trying to say, "Dress for the job you want and not the job you have." I thought about how dress shirts and ties were completely out of place in the school Jake was attending. Finally, it dawned on me the real reason Jake wore ties to school. He felt totally different from others, so his outside had to match the way he felt inside.

Mentors

Although Jake was showing improvements in some areas, he still did not give his best effort with written work or any assignment that lacked meaning for him. After discussing his desire to be an attorney, I had an important realization: Jake needed a mentor to help him understand how the "process" of school would help him reach his desired goals. I realized Jake's teachers and parents could not support all his needs. Finding an adult mentor, possibly an attorney, who could visit our school two or three times per month to work with Jake might be exactly what he needed.

After discussing the idea with my principal, I found a local attorney who volunteered as a tutor in the district. He was open to the idea of meeting a smart boy who aspired to be a lawyer, but who also needed some guidance. When educators and parents work together to take advantage of varied possibilities, they greatly increase the likelihood of keeping gifted students engaged in learning.[109] If this mentorship were to work out well, it could reroute Jake to a better path in fourth grade.

With the support of the regular classroom teacher, Jake began meeting with his mentor several times per month. He left his regular classroom during periods when his teacher and I felt he could either skip a lesson or make it up later. To observe one of the mentor sessions was like watching two old friends catch up and discuss world affairs. My principal said when she would stop by, she could not believe the questions, ideas, and thoughts coming from a nine-year old boy.

When I monitored sessions, I knew this plan was working for several reasons. First, I saw a mentor's teaching style that was compatible with a student's learning style. Then I noticed that Jake's thirst to speak was satisfied because he was interacting with a very intelligent adult. With the help of someone who had become a role model, Jake came to realize he could no longer pick and choose what he wanted to learn in school. If he wanted to achieve his goals in life, he must master spelling, writing, and organizational skills. Jake's mentor also impressed upon him that just because one has a weakness does not mean one is not smart. It simply indicates the importance of tutoring or other help until improvement is realized. When Jake heard this perspective from someone he respected, he learned to look at his situation in a different way.

If mentors are carefully selected and screened and are willing to carry out the terms of the mentorship agreement, the experience can be life-changing, as it was for Jake. Mentors can motivate young people to pursue interests and activities in fields that fit their talents.

The student also can see in the mentor an idealized self and, in that sense, realize the possibility for future accomplishments. Mentors can guide, advise, and bring clarity to making good decisions about academic direction and career path.[110] Male mentoring can also offer other beneficial effects on boys because:

- The disproportionately large number of female educators in our school systems means that boys usually are being taught by women. Women are wonderful teachers, but the male perspective and role-modeling for boys often is missing.

- Boys with positive male role models are more likely than non-mentored boys to enjoy school and believe academic success is important.
- The companionship of an adult mentor may be of great value to gifted young men, as they often find relationships with same-age peers to be unsatisfactory.
- As gifted students exhaust the educational programs at their schools, mentoring becomes a good supplement.
- Mentorships allow students the opportunity to explore interests in depth and to feel more in control of their own learning.
- Gifted students need mentors when they have interests their peers are not ready to explore. They enjoy special contact with others who have mutual interests.[111]
- Mentors can change students from reactive to proactive learners.[112]

A Big Question: To Whole-Grade Skip, or Not

As Jake's school year ended, I received a phone call from his mother. She asked if it would be possible for her son to skip fifth grade. She mentioned several reasons why she made this request, but the bottom line was she felt her son had had few learning opportunities in fourth grade and wanted to avoid the same thing in fifth grade. Except for gifted classes and an effective mentorship during fourth grade, she had watched her son slowly lose his passion for school. Accelerating to sixth grade seemed to be the best opportunity for him to be presented appropriate levels of academic challenge. I explained that this would require the school district to gather detailed information before the decision could be made.

The *Iowa Acceleration Scale*[113] would help guide the child study team through an assessment and discussion of Jake's academic and social characteristics. Elements including academic ability, aptitude, achievement, developmental factors, interpersonal skills, attitude, and support were all evaluated on a rating scale. Although the district had an acceleration policy in place, I made sure Jake's mother understood that there was not universal support for grade-skipping. I wanted her to be prepared for push-back from administrators. With a determined smile on her face she said, "Let's get started."

Since we were at the end of the school year and I felt strongly Jake was an exceptional candidate for this intervention, I discussed expediting the data collection so the Intervention Assistance Team (IAT) could meet before the last day of school. After it was agreed Jake's case was a priority, I went to work gathering the information necessary to complete the Iowa Acceleration Scale. Based on the remarks of teachers, past and present, Jake was rated strong in all target areas. Nonetheless, I had some trepidation about attitude and support with teachers, counselors, and principals as Jake entered middle school. I met with several people at the middle school and was gratified that everyone understood why some students required an acceleration, even for a gifted child who was 2e. One teacher told me she wished she had had the opportunity when she was younger.

At the final IAT meeting, the curriculum director for the school district went over the data and told Jake's family he was a very strong candidate for whole-grade acceleration. Before putting her stamp of approval on the decision, however, she cautioned that parents should always consider the repercussions of their child working with older students. For example, at the middle school level, Jake might hear inappropriate language or conversations. In high school, Jake would have to wait to do some things his peers would be doing, such as dating and driving a car.

Jake's mother explained that she had discussed these issues with her son and other family members, but they were not dissuaded from this important decision. When Jake was brought in to meet the team, he told everyone he was not scared about skipping a grade because "nothing is more frightening than being in a class that offers me nothing but a place to go each day." I had tears in my eyes when I heard him speak so directly about his frustrations and his hopes.

The curriculum director told Jake he was a great candidate for whole-grade acceleration, so he would skip from fourth to sixth grade in the fall. I saw the once-yellow flashing light turn green. Jake was not going to be held back anymore. He looked each team member in the eye and said, "I'm ready. Thank you!"

A Note from the Fourth Grade Teacher:

This was my first year of teaching. I had no idea what I was stepping into working with gifted children. I thought it would be easy, but I was wrong. I did not realize these students would require so much extra planning. I was not prepared at all. But I was happy to work with our gifted interventionist who helped me with differentiating for my smart students. She also helped me understand the social and emotional aspects of working with gifted kids.

Along my journey, it surprised me that smart children could have problems with certain areas of school. Jake had issues with writing. He did not care to edit his work and it was very sloppy and hard to read. When Jake would not even try to make his work better, it caused struggles between us.

I think providing Jake with a mentor really helped him. He seemed to enjoy the interaction, since he preferred conversations with adults over students his own age.

This year taught me never to rely on my personal beliefs about any group of children. I also feel all teachers should be better prepared to work with every type of student, so their year is more productive. There are times I wished I had not been assigned the gifted cluster group of kids my first year of teaching. However, the experience taught me more than I learned in some of my college classes. I will never forget it.

Jake's Reflections:

There were a couple things I remember quite vividly about second grade. For some reason, I remember being asked to use a ruler for a math assessment and being bothered because I didn't know if I was supposed to measure from the beginning of the ruler or the first mark on it. I also remember being asked to select a book to read from a huge shelf in the classroom and hating it. I knew I had no interest in reading. I also hated handwriting and spelling. It was in second grade I remember being engaged in some sort of reading intervention class with a special reading teacher. I remember I was not upset about having to attend this class or not being able to write well. It wasn't until later my poor writing skills finally caught up with me in school.

I don't remember a lot about third grade. However, I am glad I started to learn how to keyboard because it helped me with writing. Also, I remember an incident in which I drew a picture about a student I did not like. My third-grade teacher saw it and disciplined me for my actions. I also remember third grade was when I was identified gifted. I was very happy to attend the gifted classes and I wish I could have spent more time there than my regular classroom. I continued to see a reading specialist to help with reading skills.

Fourth grade is very clear to my memory. Socially, things were starting to get hard. I was having difficulty relating to my friends, even though some of them were also gifted kids. I also remember flying through material taught in class. A good example was when the class was struggling with long division. I could already do it perfectly because my grandfather taught it to me earlier. I also remember a parent conference at which the teacher told my mother I talked too much. I never realized this was a problem before.

This was the year I remember spending a lot of time with my gifted teacher in her pull-out classes. Because I had so much downtime in my regular classroom, I often asked if I could spend more time there. I remember it was during the second half of the school year I asked my family and gifted teacher if I could skip fifth grade. I thought it would not be any harder than sitting in fourth grade all year wasting my time.

I practiced keyboarding more this year. I usually don't like things that I must practice, but I knew this skill would help me with my writing. I am so glad I did because keyboarding is one of my most valuable skills to this day.

Finally, it was fourth grade when I met with a mentor several times a month. I respected him and listened when he said I could not decide what curriculum I wanted to learn. I had to work on spelling and writing whether I wanted to or not. I enjoyed the experience of having a mentor because it provided an opportunity to talk with someone who understood me and to learn in ways I never did in my classroom.

If Jake's first teachers in school had been asked if they thought one day he would skip a whole grade and finish number one in his high school graduating class, they probably would have answered that it was not likely. His language disability was severe enough in primary school to warrant concern from teachers and parents. Some adults felt he would never catch up with his peers despite his other gifts and talents. We should never underestimate twice-exceptional students, like Jake, because with the proper support they will soar.

7.1. Road Trip Assistance for Students like Jake

Roadblock	RoadMap	Destination
Students show signs of psychomotor over-excitability.	**Teachers and parents:** • Allow time for physical (or verbal) activity before, during and after normal daily and school activities. • Build activity and movement into children's lives. (e.g., move around while listening to audiobooks or podcasts.) • Be aware of misdiagnoses of ADHD. (ADHD is a disorder of the brain while psychomotor overexcitability points to a highly sensitive neuromuscular system.)[114] • Should not attempt to work overexcitabilities out of children. • Help children determine which environmental factors are triggers so they can anticipate situations.	**Students:** • Desire to move and speak at school and home is met. • Feel adults understand and respect their intensities as part of their giftedness by allowing movement-based activities that provide a physical release. • Understand overexcitabilities are as asset.

Students are diagnosed with language-based learning disabilities. (e.g., reading and writing.)	**Teachers:** • Provide small group/ individual reading instruction to work on targeted skills. • Provide one-to-one guidance with handwriting. • Allow younger students to tape record their stories or provide a scribe. • Allow older children to choose format for writing that is most comfortable.	**Students:** • Make improvements in reading/writing and achieve success at grade level. • Handwriting becomes more legible. • Complete quality work. • Develop a strong sense of efficacy.
Students are frustrated they cannot move at a faster pace in school.	**Teachers:** • Arrange for advanced students to work with other advanced students (pairs, groups, across classes). • Are flexible and accommodate instructional pace. (e.g., compacting, independent studies, creative thinking activities). • Allow students to set learning goals. • Allow students the chance to explore their interests. • Consider acceleration (content-and grade-based) if it is appropriate.	**Students:** • Are engaged and involved in deep level learning. • Experience continuous learning and success. • Are self-directed, excited, and focused when presented with rigorous new challenges.

Students' strong verbal ability causes excessive talking.	**Teachers:** • Appropriately challenge students so they are fully engaged in learning. • Create opportunities for students to share topics of interest in groups and to the class. **Teachers and parents:** • Teach the skill of "turn talking" or back and forth conversation. • Look for opportunities for children to capitalize on their strength for talking. (e.g., Tournament of Minds, mock trial, debate, drama.) • Avoid making talking a bad thing.	**Students:** • Express their thoughts and knowledge during appropriate times. • Find enjoyment by being challenged in school. • Understand strong verbal ability is a talent that should be nurtured. • Engaged in activities of interest that satisfy their need to use strong language skills.
Schools use only one ability test to identify gifted students leaving many smart students unidentified.	**Teachers:** • Use multiple criteria to look for students with gifts and talents. (e.g., indicators of students' cognitive abilities, academic achievement, performance in a variety of settings, interests, creativity, motivation, and learning characteristics/ behaviors)115 • Periodically review the identification process to make sure that it is valid for the population being served and the types of services being offered.	**Students:** • Are identified and receive services they need to thrive in school.

(cont.)	**Teachers:** • Ensure that standardized measures used normative sample appropriate to the students being tested, considering factors such as ethnicity, language, or the presence of a disability. (Some smart students may be twice-exceptional.) • Continue ongoing screening to allow for identification throughout the school year.	
Inexperienced teachers are assigned the gifted cluster groups of students.	**Teachers:** • Access books, websites, professional development seminars, webinars to become familiar with the characteristics of intellectually gifted students.116 • Understand curriculum based on development and ability is far more effective than curriculum based on age. • Offer students the opportunity to utilize higher-level thinking skills like analysis, synthesis, and evaluation. • Are flexible and willing to make accommodations to meet their students' special needs. • Work closely with gifted interventionists, if available. • Offer to collaborate with parents, rather than resist them, to see that children's needs are met.	**Teachers:** • Learn to understand the academic, social, and emotional needs of gifted students. • Become a part of a team (with parents and interventionists) to support and advocate for gifted students. • Make the necessary accommodations by ensuring task demands and assessments are content rich. • Find other gifted students and create opportunities for them to work together if gifted education programs are not available.

Students have desire to be exposed to career fields and more in-depth conversations than classroom or home experiences can provide.	**Teachers and parents:** • Arrange for suitable mentors in the fields of students' interests. • Talk to children about what they want to get out of mentoring relationship and what will make them feel most supported. • Set clear and realistic expectations for both the mentors and children.	**Students:** • Are guided and encouraged by adults who share expertise in common areas of interest; mentors also provide emotional connections that are nurturing to both parties. • Get glimpses of real-life experiences that may give them the challenge and motivation the need to focus and achieve.

Part III
For Parents and Teachers

Chapter 8
Intervention Specialists What They Do...and Why

A New Field

Where were the intervention specialists when I was growing up in the '60s and 70s? Even as a student, I realized there were always a few children in my classes who struggled to read and master other grade level concepts. Likewise, there were children who worked well above their peers in subjects such as reading and math. But we didn't have additional teachers (interventionists) in our classrooms providing support for students with special needs.

I expect my teachers did their very best to find ways to help their students, regardless of where they were on the learning curve. If I could go back in time and ask my third-grade teacher how she met every student's needs in our class, I am sure I would hear her say the same thing teachers today say, "It's impossible." The solution then was generally to give the struggling students extra time with the teacher to master deficiencies and to allow the smart kids to be tutors for other children or assign them more work to keep them busy.

There have been some significant changes since I walked into my first classroom. One of the biggest adjustments teachers have had to make is accommodating achievement testing. Prior to the 1983 document *A Nation at Risk*,[117] published by President Reagan's National Commission on Excellence in Education, schools administered "low stakes" tests to determine a student's progress. The results mattered only to the teacher and the student. But as data was released by Reagan's Secretary of Education, Terrell Bell, regarding the quality of teaching and learning at all levels in private and public schools, it was evident things were going to have to change in American schools. The findings in the report were anything but stellar and the first sentence said it all: "Our nation is at risk." It wasn't long before more pressure was placed on educators to provide the higher rate of success demanded by their districts, states, and the nation. They did so in the form of "high-stakes" tests. Students' achievement results were published for public review, and each teacher's and administrator's yearly evaluation was tied to the progress of their students. Some people felt *A Nation at Risk* finally put a spotlight on the need for improvements in the form of more rigorous and measurable standards.

Others felt high-stakes testing came from misguided government officials who were trying to prove the efficacy of various methods of education. Some believed that the tests were a gold mine for 'test prep' companies who were solidly behind this type of testing.

Disciplines such as art, physical education, and music were removed from some schools so the children could be more rigorously prepared for the mandated high-stakes examinations. Even recess was taken away from some struggling students so they could spend more time practicing for the tests. The decision to remove important classes so more time could be devoted to test preparation was not good for any child. It was also during this period that intervention specialists such as reading tutors and special education teachers were slowly added to many staff rosters to support the regular education teachers. These specialists work directly with children who are falling behind in reading, math, and language arts.

Washington's Attempts to Set Standards

Education in America has always been an important topic of conversation and those discussions have often been heated. Whether the debates are between career educators, lawmakers, or everyday tax-paying citizens, everyone has an opinion about what schools should look like and how they should help all students reach their potential. From as far back as 1965, when the United States government enacted the *Elementary and Secondary Education Act* (ESEA) as part of the Johnson Administration's War on Poverty, we have witnessed the need to help different populations of students who don't get a fair deal in the public education system. During the '60s, it was clear that inequity in the classroom had become a growing concern. ESEA authorized state-run programs for eligible school districts that were eager to raise the academic achievement of their struggling learners. This important government act also addressed the complex challenges that arose from challenges such as poverty, mobility problems, learning difficulties, and language deficiencies.

ESEA has been reauthorized many times since 1965. In 2002, it was reincarnated as the *No Child Left Behind Act* (NCLB). School districts within each state were held more accountable for student achievement. As part of the revisions in this act, schools had to make adequate yearly progress toward increasing their proficiency targets.

It was during this period that school boards across the country realized hiring more intervention specialists to work with regular education teachers was a necessity. However, these interventionists were trained to support only the children working below grade level, not those working at advanced levels. Therefore, the gifted and talented children were, in fact, "left behind" because states were required to provide detailed information to the government only about students performing at proficiency or below.

After more than fifteen years of evaluating whether NCLB achieved its desired goals, most educators and lawmakers felt it had fallen short. A major reason this federal law did not succeed was that it required states and districts to implement the same set of interventions, which allowed test scores to drown out individual needs and accomplishments not evaluated by standardized testing. Teachers everywhere knew mass reforms were unlikely to work. We watched too many schools be punished for failures instead of rewarded for successes. Test scores were the focus, instead of individual student growth. It was also frustrating that school districts did not report adequate achievement data on students at every level of achievement, especially those who were gifted. Twice-exceptional students were being left behind even more than those who were just "gifted."

Fortunately, the Department of Education realized that the 'one size fits all' reforms must change. President Obama authorized yet another version of the ESEA in December of 2015. This *Every Student Succeeds Act* (ESSA)[118] outlined a more flexible approach that would consider the specific needs of each community. This law seeks to help underperforming students and schools. High-ability students will now be recognized as a subgroup, and efforts will be made to assure that students of high potential are guided to be high achievers, regardless of their background.

How does this help 2e students? The *ESSA* retained the Javits Gifted and Talented Students Education program. This program focuses on identifying and serving students who are traditionally underrepresented in gifted and talented programs. It seeks to direct grant funds to children who are a minority, economically disadvantaged, English language learners, or have disabilities. The goal is to help reduce gaps in achievement and to encourage the establishment of equal educational opportunities for all students. Also, for the first time, ESSA specifically notes that school districts may use Title I funds (federal money for elementary and secondary education programs to focus on special needs populations) to identify and serve gifted and talented students.[119]

As part of ESSA, provisions called *To Aid Gifted and High-Ability Learners by Empowering the Nations Teacher's Act* (TALENT) have been integrated into the new education law to address meeting the needs of gifted learners and those with the potential to achieve at high levels.

Key provisions in ESSA for the gifted population require that states and school districts must now report student data at each achievement level, not just those performing at or below proficiency. Also, each state must disaggregate this data by student subgroups-for example race, low-income, and gender. School districts that apply for government professional development funds must include their plans to improve the skills of teachers and other school leaders so they can be prepared to identify gifted and talented students, and provide appropriate instructional practices such as enrichment, acceleration, curriculum compacting, dual enrollment, and early entrance to kindergarten. If your school district received professional development funds through ESSA, parents and teachers must be sure that educators are trained to identify 2e children and provide instruction for their specialized needs. With these provisions now included in federal law for the first time, we hope that schools will do a better job of addressing the unique needs of gifted and high potential learners from all races and socioeconomic groups.

It is important to realize that while ESSA is currently the law of the land and gives a great deal of responsibility and accountability to the states, by 2020 the Department of Education's K-12 education budget was reduced by 10%, or 7.1 billion dollars from the previous year.[120] So it is hard to say what portions of ESSA will be funded. Currently, there is discussion about eliminating the Act altogether; but that is unlikely, because ESSA is the latest version of laws that have been around for decades. Nonetheless, as education budgets continue to be cut, the future effectiveness of ESSA is unclear.

Even if ESSA remains in place and schools across the country are able to work towards doing a better job of serving their gifted and talented learners, I am still concerned that regular education teachers, like those of the previous decades, have too much on their plate to live up to ESSA requirements. Most teachers still have the demands of bringing low-performing children up to grade level, planning appropriate challenges for high-potential learners, and supporting those students with social and emotional concerns. Without support from intervention specialists, this can become overwhelming very quickly. When classrooms must include 2e students, regular education teachers require the support of both knowledgeable *special* education and *gifted* education teachers. It is not enough to address one side of this child's academic needs and ignore the other. Administrators must consider both gifted and special education interventionists as essential to a well-rounded school staff.

When I became a gifted interventionist many years ago, I was fortunate to work in a school district that believed every school should have at least one part-time or full-time gifted specialist in their building to serve the gifted students. During the periods I spent with my students, I made sure they were offered rigorous opportunities to strengthen critical and creative thinking skills. Nonetheless, I knew the limited time I worked with these children would never be enough to challenge them appropriately in school. These children are gifted all day every day, and often need more extra help than is offered.

In response to this, I became a partner with the regular classroom teacher to help set goals, prepare lesson plans, and evaluate student work in the regular classroom. Sometimes I joined the teaching team, because I knew that the regular classroom teachers didn't have the time or, in some cases, the knowledge and training to differentiate for the advanced students in their classes. I showed teachers how to identify high-potential students because those special talents are not always apparent.

After becoming a specialist, I wanted to speak with larger audiences about gifted children. I enjoyed the opportunity to help K-12 staff understand that smart children have special social and emotional needs which, if not properly addressed, could lead to difficulties in school. I was encouraged when school leaders realized they had knowledgeable specialists in their own district to provide the appropriate professional development for their teachers.

As the consulting part of my job grew, I wondered why so many teachers and counselors were not more prepared to effectively work with the high potential children in their schools. Although the National Association for Gifted Children was founded in 1954 and Congress passed the Javits Gifted and Talented Act in 1988, I realized that few universities required students seeking education degrees to complete an undergraduate course in gifted education. This deficiency will challenge every teacher because, without specialists, smart students receive most of their instruction in the regular classroom.

Why So Few Gifted Interventionists?

It has been my experience teaching in several states that gifted interventionists seem to be the most overlooked staff members. When they are hired, they generally serve more than one school, and so they don't seem to be an integral part of the educational process for students. Because the specialists must travel to multiple schools in a day or week, their time in each school and the effectiveness of their services are limited.

Additionally, school district budget issues may mean that the interventionist is one of the last teachers to be hired, if one is hired at all. When staff cuts come, the gifted interventionists are generally among the first to go. These cuts deprive the over three million academically gifted and talented students in the United States who need extra help.

Adding to the general confusion is the fact that because there is no federal mandate to identify and serve high-potential children, states are left to decide the direction their schools will take regarding appropriate policy developments. Some states support identification and services, while others do not. The NAGC 2018-2019 *State of the States Report in Gifted Education*[121] noted that 38 states require the identification of gifted and talented students. When states were asked whether gifted programming services were mandated, 24 states reported a law or rule mandating gifted programming options, 15 states indicated no mandate, and 11 states indicated it was determined by local education agencies. If a state is one that authorizes identification but does not have a clear policy about how to serve their gifted students, then each individual district will decide the actual programs and services to be offered to their brightest students.

In many school districts, these can range from early entrance to kindergarten, cluster grouping within regular classrooms, gifted resource rooms, AP classes in high school, and/or dual enrollment. These are good options for special educational services, but very few include a licensed gifted interventionist who works directly with the students.

Accountability for gifted students and the teachers who work with them varies widely. Because some states do not have a policy for identifying gifted children, it is hard to know how many gifted children exist in each state. If we identify gifted children in a district but do not provide services, we cannot know clearly whether the child's education includes support for their special needs. If states receive funding for gifted education but have no accountability for how the money is used in their districts, the funds could easily be diverted to other purposes. We are fortunate that ESSA, if not watered down, will hold districts within each state accountable when they apply for Title I funds[122] pertaining to gifted education, particularly when teaching twice-exceptional students.

As a member of my state association for gifted children, I receive *Advocacy Alert* emails with state board of education updates on achievement in gifted education. There is one clear message I often take away from these emails. Those who make the important decisions in our schools still have very different views of what gifted services should be, and they question who should decide what the standards of quality are for this group of children. (As for twice-exceptional students, many of these same individuals still don't believe a gifted child can have a disability or a child with a disability can be gifted. If the 2e child is identified, then the question becomes, "Should we only help the child with their disability, or should we only focus on their gifts and talents?") The conversation goes back and forth with much uncertainty. Should schools hire gifted interventionists to work with their identified students? Would a gifted consultant be a good fit to work with teachers who need help identifying their high potential and 2e students, and help teach them in their regular education classrooms? Or should a district merely cluster group their high-potential children in a classroom to be taught by a teacher with no background in gifted education, and call it "service"?

Gifted Education by My State

By law, Ohio's school districts are required to identify students as gifted in grades K-12, but they are not required to serve gifted children.[123] This disappointing fact shows just how important it is for parents of gifted children to educate themselves about the need for gifted services in all schools and then lobby administrators and legislatures to make positive changes in their districts and states.[124]

The state board of education leaves it up to each school district to develop a plan for the services of gifted students. A good, gifted program provides many options for students, and Ohio encourages that a continuum of services be provided by each district board of education.[125] These may include but are not limited to the following.

1. A differentiated curriculum
2. Cluster grouping of gifted students in a regular classroom
3. Mentorships

4. Accelerated course work
5. Dual enrollment opportunities including but not limited to College Credit Plus
6. Advanced Placement courses
7. Honors courses
8. International Baccalaureate course
9. Magnet schools
10. Self-contained gifted classrooms with a gifted specialist as the teacher of record
11. A single-subject class where the gifted specialist is the teacher of record
12. Pull-out gifted resource rooms
13. Independent study
14. Services through a trained Arts instructor.

When Ohio revised the Gifted Operating Standards in March 2017[126,] school districts discovered they had increased flexibility how to serve gifted children. This includes the ability to hire gifted specialists to work directly in schools. The hiring of these interventionists has been on the decline for many years in Ohio, which is unfortunate because classroom teachers in my state are provided no training to understand, identify, or provide special services to gifted children. The Gifted Operating Standards do encourage districts to provide training for regular education teachers who provide services to gifted children, with a minimum of 30 hours of gifted education training.

In place of a mandate to accommodate gifted students, the Ohio Department of Education (ODE) added a "gifted performance indicator" to their state report card in 2012. According to ODE, "The Gifted Indicator reflects the level of services to, and the performance of, students who are identified gifted."[127] The Gifted Indicator is a "Met" or "Not Met" determination that requires a district or school to obtain a minimum threshold on each of three components: 1) Performance (determined by the *Gifted Performance Index*); 2) Progress (determined by the *Gifted Value-Added* letter grade; 3) Inputs (determined by a total point score connected to various measure of gifted identification and service).[128] Districts must satisfy each of the components to merit the *overall* gifted performance indicator. When the state report card is published each year, the public can see if a district has "met" the requirements for accommodating gifted children.

In 2016, the first year that the gifted performance indicator was fully phased in, only 12 out of over 600 Ohio school districts met all three components in the gifted indicator. As of 2018, 38 out of 609 school districts "met" this indicator.[129] Some progress has been made improving service to gifted students, but it is still unsatisfactory. One reason for this is that gifted students are less likely to be identified in poorer rural districts, small towns, and urban districts. When these students are identified as gifted, they are restricted to the regular classroom with no cluster grouping and no support from a gifted intervention specialist. (As of May 2022, Ohio's State Report Card will reflect changes in the gifted performance indicator to better reflect state gifted policy goals. See oagc.com for these changes.)

Making the Right Decisions

During my career, I have seen the positive effect of state and district education policy on how teachers teach and how students learn. But there is still more work to be done in establishing a gifted education policy that helps all students thrive. As stated by former NAGC president Dr. Sally Krisel, "Gifted education policies provide a framework for identification, services, teacher preparedness, and accountability for student learning and program evaluation, which together should define comprehensive, equitable opportunities for high achieving and high potential students."[130]

Now that ESSA is on the minds of school districts across the country, the plan to use government funds to train educators to work with gifted children should focus on getting the best return for these important dollars. Those in charge of making these decisions should consider this valuable option: hire a gifted intervention specialist to work in each school. This strategy can ensure the long-term benefits that regular teaching services will not provide. When schools include a full-time gifted specialist, this individual not only provides support for the high-potential children in the school, but also supports teachers and parents.

Using ESSA funds to train teachers to identify and work with gifted students is important. But it is just as important to hire a knowledgeable staff member who has an advanced degree in gifted education to work every day with regular education staff. This commitment by school districts ensures there will be follow-through with the planning for high-potential children. I stress this point with parents: one would expect a trained specialist to help with a child's physical health concerns, so a parent should expect nothing less than a knowledgeable specialist in their child's school who can help with the needs of 2e children.

Finally, as we unpack the diverse state mandates across the country and the many district budget woes affecting how we serve our gifted children, the final reason for the lack of gifted interventionists in our schools is very simple: there is still a prevailing belief that these students will survive in school without additional support.

It is simply incorrect that smart children will learn on their own without differentiated curricula, adjusted materials and strategies, or accelerated and modified schedules to meet their academic, social, and emotional needs. When I encounter someone with this philosophy, I tell them about a digital technology class I took many years ago.

My school district arranged for twenty teachers to meet during several school days to learn about digital technologies to help with classroom instruction. These included blogs (a type of website where content is presented in reverse chronological order and information is presented in a conversational style) and wikis (a type of website or online resource that can be edited by multiple users). From the first day of class, it was obvious there were some teachers who were the "smart ones." They had been using digital technology in their classes for months. But they wanted to learn more, so they registered for the class. And just like any classroom, there were a few teachers who barely knew how to use a computer at all.

After we received the syllabus for the class, our instructor administered a pre-test to determine how she would handle instruction. It identified those who needed to move quickly, so they could compact some of the assignments; and those who needed more time to learn the different types of technology, so they could set their own pace. The technology instructor even considered the learning styles and grade levels her teacher-students taught as she planned the projects for our technology classes.

When this course ended, I had not only learned some great digital technology to use with my students, but I had also experienced a great demonstration of one-size-does-*not*-fit-all instruction. The teacher-students who finished at a faster pace flourished, while the 'regular' students finished on time and with adequate comprehension.

What the Interventionist Does

Note: After losing my job as a gifted interventionist in a former school district due to a failed tax levy, it became clear that gifted education did not seem important to the administrators and school board members who eliminated gifted services from their K-12 schools. The overwhelming feeling the gifted students, their families, and I got from this decision was "those students will be just fine without any special services and support." Because of this erroneous misunderstanding, I felt it important to describe the work of a gifted education program, and to make it clear that hiring gifted specialists offers the "best bang for the buck" in a school budget, to ensure "all" children's needs are met.

For an individual trained to be part of the big picture in a child's school career, a job in gifted education is a calling. It requires great flexibility and patience because the job can feel as though one is on an island all alone. Just like the parent of a gifted child who confides in others and gets an unsympathetic response, I too have received remarks from individuals that indicate a lack of understanding of what I do as a gifted intervention specialist. I was once told that "it must be fun to play games all day with those smart kids!" I certainly don't play games all day. My job comes with high pressure and the responsibility to 'get it right' for the smart children, who don't have many people advocating for them in their day-to-day school experiences. It is more than just working directly with gifted children.

I am responsible for writing curricula, collaborating with teachers on projects, and consulting with parents about gifted issues. Each is important to the success of a high-potential child.

Whether I'm working in a regular classroom as a teaching partner, or teaching students in another setting, I am responsible for creating opportunities to improve the convergent and divergent thinking skills of talented students. The curriculum I develop, using the National Standards in Gifted and Talented Education, is always of high interest and involves solving real-world problems. It is music to my ears each week to hear my students express how happy and excited they are to explore meaningful and challenging assignments. They crave rigorous and in-depth learning experiences that allow them to think critically and generate unique solutions to problems. They are often willing to give up part of their weekends to do their work. One of the twice-exceptional boys in this book told me he would gladly come to school on Saturdays if it meant he got the chance to engage in activities like the ones in his gifted education classes. Those experiences helped him understand that although he was 2e, he was not broken. This smart boy quickly discovered he had strengths and could certainly overcome his weaknesses to reach full potential.

I enjoy collaborating with colleagues at each grade level in their school. Sometimes this can take up to fifty percent of my time, depending on how much help the regular classroom teachers want and need. Each teacher with a cluster group of gifted students receives support. This can be guidance when selecting teaching strategies and materials for gifted students, or helping a teacher compact a unit for students who have pretested and demonstrated competency for skills that will be taught.

I can assist a teacher by providing instruction on how to tier assignments for different levels of ability in a classroom or create activities that cause the gifted child to process important ideas at a higher level. Overall, my experience in collaborating with other educators has resulted in more understanding about gifted children in the schools. Teachers learn that the behavioral issues that arise can be ameliorated because, as author and educator Carol Ann Tomlinson once said, "The students' big appetites for knowing are being satisfied."

Working with parents of gifted children is very rewarding. They often don't have anywhere else to turn to discuss their child's special needs. As I wrote about the four smart boys in this book, I remembered that all the parents were at one time or another very frustrated with the education their boys were (or were not) receiving. The 'traffic jams' they encountered were varied, but all were stressful. As an advocate for their children, I helped untangle some of the problems they experienced by finding solutions that were available in each boy's school.

From making sure a child is matched with the right classroom teacher, to promoting different types of acceleration, I make sure principals and teachers are aware of the student's needs. In some cases, simply listening to a mother or father's concerns is enough to energize the parent to speak up for their child in ways they might not have considered before. The biggest reward I receive from working with the families of gifted children is hearing them tell me they finally understand what it means to be an advocate for their child. They realize they can move forward in a calm, informed manner and take proactive steps to create support for their child's needs, even if sometimes they are met with resistance and criticism.

The Conversations Must Continue

The positive strides in American education over the past several decades should not be overlooked. Implementing research-based learning strategies, integrating technology into classroom instruction, and establishing accountability for teachers and students are all steps in the right direction to improve our schools. This alone is not enough. As the conversations continue locally and nationally about how to reform American education so *all* children have a chance to achieve at their highest levels, we must be clear that there is still a long road ahead. When certain groups of students are still misjudged and not adequately supported, we have a problem. When America's top students do not perform well compared to their counterparts around the world, we have a problem.

Our education system in the United States needs to adapt to a fast-changing world. There is no excuse for a child to be held back from achieving because they are not properly supported in the schools. As authors Norm Augustine and Rudy Crew noted, "This is our Sputnik moment. The challenge is that the demands our children face today are being dictated by a world in which change comes rapidly and leaving talent on the table will put our nation at risk, leaving us all behind."[131] Funding education budgets adequately, enacting federal service mandates for high-potential children, and providing trained gifted interventionists in all schools are steps we must take to ensure all students are supported.

Chapter 9
Hints and Helps for Parents and Teaching 2e Boys

Intensity, hands-on learning, curiosity, and coping skills are important in the lives of all gifted boys. They are especially important to understand in 2e boys, because when they are addressed, the boy is more likely to succeed in areas of weakness. In Mateo, Jamal, Melvin, and Jake's stories, parents and teachers helped turn their lives from sad and disappointing to happy and more satisfied simply by focusing on the helpful suggestions offered by professionals in gifted education.

Emotional Intensity

I have mentioned throughout this book the intensity of gifted children. They think and feel deeply, and often differently, than other children. This may be especially true of 2e boys, who are wrestling not only with their giftedness, but also with feelings of inadequacy, shame, and other negative emotions. They give little value to those things they can do well because it comes easily to them, and instead they focus on what they cannot do as well as their peers. Parents and teachers may repeatedly criticize them for "not trying hard enough" in those areas, failing to recognize that these 2e children are developing with conditions that make learning and achievement more difficult. Strategies that might work for a typical child's development could otherwise be detrimental for those carrying emotional burdens. Below are some ideas that are helpful.

Table 9.1. Strategies to Support Emotional Intensity in Gifted Boys[132]

- Do not try to minimize emotions by saying things like, "You are too sensitive. You are too intense."
- Focus on coping mechanisms instead of trying to change the child.
- Help him understand that intense feelings are normal for gifted children.
- Honor the child's emotions by listening to his problems. Don't rush in to give advice.
- Reassure the child when he is afraid. Encourage journal writing, artwork, or poetry.
- Don't expect adult responsibility. He is a child, even if he is intellectually advanced. He will certainly reason like a child and demonstrate the emotional maturity of his chronological age.
- Be aware of the things he does to 'push your buttons' so you can stay calm during his outbursts.
- Validate his role in solving problems.
- Help him manage his emotions by coaching him in how to redirect his feelings before they are overwhelming. (Parents may need to learn these skills first!)
- Encourage his interests in any field he enjoys, not just those that are "masculine." Not all boys are athletes. If he enjoys sports, but shies away from teams, then perhaps tennis, swimming, diving, golf, running, and other sports can give him the advantage of challenging himself individually. If he becomes proficient and later wants to try out for a team that values individual performance rather than group skills, he's ready.
- Help both adults and children to understand that sensitivity does not mean weakness.
- Provide professional counseling when appropriate to prevent social and emotional problems.

Hands-on-Learners

Research tells us that to engage children's brains, we must allow them to move, touch, and experience in order to learn.[133] Most elementary teachers provide numerous opportunities for their students to learn through hands-on experience. My younger students always enjoyed tactile exploration, such as making picture graphs with real objects, manipulating alphabet puzzles, and using shapes to make words. I have observed a few ambitious colleagues guide their students to explain their work through tactile procedures, such as making DNA models in science class with materials of the students' choice. Jean Piaget, well-known psychologist for his pioneering work in child development, explained in his theory of cognitive development that learning comes through doing.[134]

As children get older, however, too many classrooms are reduced to mere lectures and notetaking. Unless a class is working with math manipulatives or science lab equipment, the hands-on part of school seems to disappear. Sometimes teachers feel hands-on activities cause too much noise and movement in their rooms, so they turn to less lively methods of learning new material. Many of the 2e boys, including those I interviewed for this book, said that their favorite classes involved direct interaction with the environment. They much preferred work that allowed them to create things with their hands. They complained about the number of workbook pages they had to sit and complete each day when their natural inclination was to move and manipulate materials. This is particularly true of boys.

In their book *The Mind of Boys*, Michael Gurian and Kathy Stevens cite research which shows that in boy's brains a larger part of the cerebral cortex is dedicated to spatial and mechanical functioning.[135] "Boys sometimes learn better through movement and pictures than by listening to words." But in many of today's classrooms, the objective is to have children reading at earlier ages and allow movement only during gym and recess. In many schools, recesses are being shortened, and physical education is considered a frill. It should not be surprising, then, that "active curious boys who are enthusiastic, hands-on learners often have trouble in the first years of schooling." [136]

Boys must be able to exercise their own learning styles, which surely includes movement, so physical activities must be included. Below are some methods to keep active boys engaged.

Table 9.2. Strategies to Support Hands-On Learning

- Allow children to participate in cooking activities.
- Use familiar materials in new ways (e.g., a deck of playing cards for math skills)
- Allow children to demonstrate their learning.
- Rhythm-clap spelling words and math facts.
- Use scavenger hunts to search for items related to a unit study.
- Allow students to perform plays or skits to demonstrate historical events/scenes from books.
- Make graphs/Venn diagrams with real objects or even people.
- Incorporate more S.T.E.M. learning units in the classroom.137
- Include tangrams, pattern blocks, dice, coins, and geoboards in math explorations.
- Create 3-D maps with paper, clay, textured fabrics, and materials.
- Use a cookie sheet filled with colored sand or salt to allow the child to write letters, words or math facts. This provides a tactile experience unlike that of paper and pencil.
- Color code parts of writing with highlighters, gel pens, colored pencils.
- Use interactive displays and collections.

Curiosity and Questioning

Parents and teachers can wonder about the difference between a bright child and one who is gifted. Truly gifted children tend to be intensely curious and to ask a myriad of questions that usually demonstrate higher-level thinking, compared to the curiosity of other students. Because gifted children already possess a good deal of information about many topics, they are more ready to use and manipulate that information.

I had a 2e student who, when exploring complicated math problems, would sometimes put down his pencil, stare at the ceiling, and say, "Give me a minute. I'm thinking." Then he would ask a question, or more likely several questions. It could feel like a tennis match as information volleyed back and forth.

The curiosity of gifted children can become problematic when they must narrow their many interests to a single topic or idea to study for a class project: picking just one can feel limiting. When a topic is finally selected, the child may have difficulty finishing the assignment because he wants to dig deeper into the content. Deadlines may have to be extended to allow a gifted child to finish the assignment to his satisfaction. Sometimes a child can be excused from work in areas of strength to afford time to complete the more challenging project.

The following strategies have provided great success for my twice-exceptional students. By supporting their need to be curious and ask lots of questions, they are able to be more adventurous in their learning and feel more confident in school.

Table 9.3. Strategies to Support Questioning and Curiosity

Questioning	Curiosity
Be accepting of all points of view whether the answer is correct, vague, or wondering (the student makes a connection in their head about something they are learning and they say it out loud). Students then feel comfortable answering without fear of ridicule.	Create a room that invites inquiry (pictures, books, areas for music, art; provide a variety of materials for self-initiated projects.
Provide reflection times so students can continue to formulate, ask, and discuss more questions.	Be understanding about how high levels of independent thinking can lead students to question authority and adults to label a child as difficult. While discipline may be necessary, punishment usually is not.

Questioning	**Curiosity**
Utilize the "four corner" questioning strategy. This approach asks students to make a decision about a problem or question. Each of the four corners of the classroom is labeled with a different response (strongly agree, agree, disagree, strongly disagree. Students move to the corner that best aligns with their thinking.	Teach children how to safely look for the answers to their questions. • Make sure "Safe Search" is activated on Google or Bing. • Utilize age-appropriate search engines like Kiddle (ages 5+); KidzSearch (ages 10+); RefSeek (ages 12+); Internet Public Library Kidspace (age 8+); KidInfo (ages K-12).
Use "think, pair, share" method when questioning: Arrange students in pairs. 1) Ask a question. 2) Offer time to think. 3) Partners share their own answers, and then discuss with the class.	Don't micromanage children. Allow them to make mistakes when exploring new areas of interest like playing an instrument or learning origami. Gifted children are often shattered when they make an error because they think they should know everything. Making mistakes should be encouraged because mastering errors builds resilience.
Use the *Socratic Method*: a form of shared dialogue between teachers and students, based on asking and answering thought provoking questions.	Don't instill fear in children that will cause them to be less curious about their world. For example, don't tell them they can't take a walk in the woods because they might find snakes there. If this is a real danger, teach them how to "see and avoid."

Questioning	Curiosity
Implement a variety of questioning tools: • Frame questions as discussions. • Read to your child books that have titles that are questions like: *Are You My Mother? What if Everybody Did That? Little Kids First Big Book of Why*. • Offer activities that encourage children to think about why and how things work. (Sand, water play, art, and music all involve the discovery process that can stimulate new questions.)	Understand that curious students can act impulsively and intensely while exploring something new.

Coping

Many gifted boys who are expected to conform, either by their families or society, will find themselves in a dilemma about how to handle their situation. Some smart boys rebel and become angry at parents and teachers because they don't want to conform to fit the mold. One former student expressed to his father that he wanted to act in school plays instead of play football, and he received negative feedback, his father attempting to mold him into something he was not. In addition to learning to cope with other people's perceptions of what is important in life, twice-exceptional boys must also learn to manage the fact that they are gifted and excel in some areas but are delayed in others. Gifted boys need different coping-mechanisms because they are likely to face different problems.[138]

The boy code (non-verbal rules and expectations that define boyhood and masculinity in America) discussed earlier is a distinct issue. This code can put many boys into a "gender straitjacket"[139] that constrains them so that they do not recognize themselves. If a boy does not have strong connections with his family, teachers, and/or friends who are willing to support his differences, he is in danger of hiding behind a mask. Once he is hidden, his real gifts and talents become hidden and thwarted. Such boys can become both angry and depressed because their true selves are hidden and disrespected.

In addition to coping with reality as he finds his way in life, a gifted boy must learn to manage the individual traits that sets him apart from peers. These super-sensitivities may be:[140]

- Intellectual, characterized by questioning so sophisticated it may stump the teacher and be unintelligible to the rest of the class.
- Emotional, exemplified by emotional extremes, anxiety, and empathy, a desire to right wrongs and to solve the world's problems.
- Sensual, displayed as a heightened awareness of sight, smell, hearing, taste, and touch. They may be bothered by the buzzing of fluorescent lights, tags in their clothes, tight waistbands or socks, or music that's too loud.
- Imaginational, characterized by a great sense of humor (that others sometimes don't understand), a love for performing, a rich fantasy life, and daydreaming.
- Psychomotor, demonstrated through very high energy, rapid speech, competitiveness, and an inability to sit still.

If teachers do not understand these overexcitabilities, they will see the child's behavior as an effort to derail classroom management, which can lead to failed discipline and further acting out.

Gifted adolescents may try to survive in their world by hiding their gifts so as to seem "normal." They want friends and fun just like other students, but they may not be able to find others with whom they are comfortable and can become lonely and sometimes desperate. With these feelings, they can become aggressive, blame others, or even harm themselves. If parents and teachers help gifted students learn and apply the coping and survival methods they need, they will begin to live more authentic and happier lives.

Table 9.4. Strategies to Support Coping with Real Life[141]

- Start early by helping the child talk about his emotions; take his issues seriously.
- Explain that his heightened sensitivities can make him more emotional than other children and that his feelings are normal, but that he must learn to recognize when he is getting out of control. The body mirrors one's emotions and feelings which are often expressed as physical symptoms, like tense stomach, sinking heart, blushing, headache, or nausea.
- Work with him on a plan for what to do when he feels overwhelmed. This should include a way to relax or redirect his energy from the intense emotions.
- Help him form a realistic view of self and abilities. Parents and teachers can help a gifted child learn about what he is good at, what he is "normal" at, and what areas are challenges for him.
- Help develop your child's tolerance for stress and frustration by exposing him to increasingly more age-appropriate challenging situations. (Older children can help set their own small and long-term goals.) The satisfaction of achievement will help the child realize he can cope with difficult situations.
- Say yes as often as you can. Gifted boys want to try new things, invent, and create, and they hear "No" far too often. Constant thwarting of curiosity builds frustration. Before you say "no", ask yourself "why not?" If the answer is still no, explain your reasons.
- Remain calm if an explosion occurs. Anger and frustration always create more anger and frustration. The adults working with the child must stay emotionally neutral. Watch your body language, too. Gifted kids know when your words and body language are incongruent, and they consider it duplicitous. Monitor body movements, facial expressions, eye contact, the volume and tone of the voice, and all other gestures that signal disapproval.

Epilogue

Working with twice-exceptional boys and their families has brought great joy to me as an educator. As I take the trip in school with each student and their family, it is a commitment to support them often for several years. Although each student I encounter is different, they all desire to be successful and valued for their individuality. The often "back and forth" attempts to support strengths as well as areas of need can become quite challenging. But the time we spend trying to get it right for these children is worth it when we see they are going to reach their potential and they are happy.

As I wrote in the preface, my journey exploring how to help 2e children began with a bright-eyed seven-year-old boy named Jake. His infectious smile and desire to learn was something I will never forget. I will also never forget the sudden downward turn he took in fourth grade when he felt school was not an accommodating place for him. I shared just a part of Jake's story here, but I often tell his whole story (second grade through high school) to parents and teachers who work with 2e boys. It helps teachers who are working with 2e students and wondering how to proceed, and it also helps parents and gives them hope for their child.

I was fortunate to work with Jake not only in elementary school, but also in middle and high school. He went on to an elite university as a commended scholar and was approaching graduation when he shared some thoughts with me. His words show that while rearing and teaching 2e boys sometimes can be confusing and frustrating, things can and <u>do</u> work out. With guidance, they do find a path that is best for them, and their lives can become very fulfilling and rewarding. Today, Jake is heading to law school, right where he always wanted to be.

Here are Jake's comments upon graduating from high school:

> *If I were to give advice to another gifted student like me, first I would say take it day by day and do not focus so much on being an adult right now. Although you may be very mature, there is still joy to be found hanging out with people your own age.*
>
> *Next, I would recommend that students should diversify their interests. Play a sport or join a club that is not just science or math oriented.*
>
> *Third, I would advise you to pick your battles wisely. Although you may be correct in principle about a matter, it's not worth getting into a heated debate about it.*
>
> *Fourth, I would tell students like me to be crazy ambitious! You have so much potential, so don't relegate yourself to mediocrity. Don't ever settle. Also, don't let your parents, teachers, or counselors think you're dreaming too big.*
>
> *Finally, focus on being happy. Don't be cocky about how smart you are because no one likes that kind of person, and you won't' make friends that way. Getting the best grades and highest test scores won't make you happy. You need more than that in your life. You need fulfilling hobbies, and good friends. Have some fun!*

I think those are wise words, and I wish you the best as you travel with your sons during their intellectual journey.

References

American Speech-Language-Hearing Association. (n.d.). *Language Based Learning Disabilities: Reading, Spelling, and Writing.* Retrieved from http://www.asha.org/public/speech/disorders/LBLD.htm#a.

Alvino, J. (1995). *Consideration and strategies for parenting the gifted child.* Retrieved from http://nrcgt.uconn.edu/research-based_resources/alvino.

Angyal, C. (2017). *Tights, tutus and relentless teasing: Inside ballet's bullying epidemic.* Retrieved from https://www.huffpost.com/entry/ballet-bullying_n_59d5148ce4b0218923e724bf.

Assouline, S., Colangelo, N., Lupowski-Shoplik, A., Lipscomb, J., & Forstadt, L. (2009). *Iowa acceleration scale: A guide for whole-grade acceleration K-8* (3rd ed.). Tucson, AZ: Great Potential Press.

Assouline, S., Colangelo, N., VanTassel-Baska, J., & Lupkowski-Shoplik, A. (Eds.). (2015). *A nation empowered: Evidence trumps the excuses holding back America's brightest students.* Retrieved from http://www.accelerationinstitute.org/nation_empowered.

Augustine, N., & Crew, R. (2016). *Leaving talent on the table: Fixing gifted education in American.* Retrieved from http://edexcellence.net/articles/leaving-talent-on-the-table-fixing-gifted-education-in-america.

Baum, S., Shader, R., & Owen, S. (2017). *To be gifted and learning disabled: Strength based strategies for helping twice-exceptional students with LD-ADHD-ASD and more* (3rd ed.). Waco, TX: Prufrock Press.

Beljan, P. (2011). Misdiagnosis of culturally diverse students. In J. A. Castellano, & A. D. Frazier (Eds.), *Special populations in gifted education: Understanding our most able students from diverse backgrounds* (pp. 317-332). Waco, TX: Prufrock Press.

Berger, S. L. (2014). *College planning for gifted students: Choosing and getting into the right college* (Updated Ed. ed.). Waco, TX: Prufrock Press.

Biddulph, S. (2013). *Raising boys: Why boys are different and how to help them become happy and well-balanced men* (3rd ed.). New York: Ten Speed Press.

Blackburn, H. (2017). The status of women in STEM in higher educaiton: A review of the literature 2007-2017. *Science & Technology Libraries*, 36(3), 235-273.

Brody, L., & Mills, C. (1997). Gifted children with learning disabilities: A review of the issues. *Journal of Learning Disabilities*, 30(2), 282-297.

Brown, A. (2017). *5 key findings about LGBT Americans*. Retrieved from https://www.pewresearch.org/fact-tank/2017/06/13/5-key-findings-about-lgbt-americans/.

Brulles, D., Brown, K. L., & Winebrenner, S. (2016). *Differentiated lessons for every learner: Standards based activities and extensions for middle school.* Waco, TX: Prufrock Press.

Bullard, J. (2017). *Creating environments for learning: Birth to age eight* (3rd ed.). Hoboken, NJ: Pearson Education Inc.

Burruss, J., & Kaenzig, L. (2011). *Introversion: The often-forgotten facor impacting the gifted.* Retrieved from http://sengifted.org/introversion-the-often-forgotten-factor-impacting-the-gifted/.

Cain, S. (2012). *Quiet: The power of introverts in a world that cannot stop talking.* New York: Crown.

Center for Parent Resources and Information. (2019). *Categories of disability under IDEA.* Retrieved from http://www.parentcenterhub.org/repository/categories.

Centers for Disease Control and Prevention. (2021). *Obsessive-compulsive disorder in children.* Retrieved from https://www.cdc.gov/childrensmentalhealth/ocd.html.

Chu, J. (2014). *When boys become boys: Developing, relationships, and masculinity.* New York: University Press.

Clark, B. (2013). *Growing up gifted: Developing the potential of children at school and at home* (8th ed.). Upper Saddle River, NJ: Pearson Prentice Hall.

Coalition of Schools Educating Boys of Color. (2021). *Gifted students.* Retrieved from http://www.coseboc.org/policy/gifted-students.

Cohn, S., & Kerr, B. (2001). *Smart boys: Talent, manhood, and the search for meaning.* Tucson, AZ: Great Potential Press.

Colangelo, N., Assouline, S., & Gross, M. (2004). *A nation deceived: How schools hold back America's brightest students* (Vol. I). Iowa City, IA: The University of Iowa.

Colorado Department of Education. (2017). *Twice-exceptional students: Gifted students with disabilities: Level 1: An introductory resource book.* Retrieved from https://www.cde.state.co.us/gt/level_1_resource_handbook_4th_ed_1-17-17.

Coyle, D. (2009). *The talent code: Greatness isn't born it's grown: Here's how.* New York: Bantam Books.

Cross, T. (2011). *Social and emotional needs: The rage of gifted students.* Retrieved from http://sengifted.org/socialemotional-needs-the-rage-of-gifted-students/.

Davis, J. (2010). *Bright, talented, and black: A guide for families of African-American learners.* Tucson, AZ: Great Potential Press.

Dawson, P., & Guare, R. (2009). *Smart but scattered: The revolutionary "executive skills" approach to helping kids reach their potential.* New York: The Guildford Press.

Deligeorge, D. (2013). *Andrygny and gifted youth.* Retrieved from https://www.sengifted.org/post/androgyny-and-gifted-youth.

Distin, K. (2006). *Gifted children: A guide for parents and professionals.* Philadelphia: Jessica Kingsley.

Dotterer, C. (2019). *Handwriting: Brain-body disconnet: Adaptive teaching techniques to unlock a child's dysgraphia for the classroom and home.* Powell, OH: Author Academcy Elite.

Dweck, C. (2007). *MIndset: The new psychology of success.* New York: Ballantine Books.

Erwin, J. (2004). *The classroom of choice: Giving students what they need and getting what you want.* Alexandria, VA: Association for Supervision and Curriculum.

Estroff, S. (n.d.). *The age-by-age guide to teaching kids time management.* Retrieved from https://www.scholastic.com/parents/family-life/parent-child/teach-kids-to-manage-time.html.

Felder, M., Taradash, G., Antoine, E., Ricci, M., Stemple, M., & Byamugisha, M. (2015). *Increasing diversity in gifted education: Research-based strategies for identification and program services.* Waco, TX: Prufrock Press.

Fiedler, E., Lange, R., & Winebrenner, S. (2002). In search of reality: Unraveling the myths about tracking, ability grouping, and the gifted. *Roeper Review,* 24, 108-111.

Fisher, D., Frey, N., Quaglia, R., Smith, D., & Lande, L. (2018). *Engagement by design: Creating learning environments where students thrive.* Thousand Oaks, CA: Corwin.

Foley-Nicpon, M., Assouline, S., & Colangelo, N. (2013). Twice-exceptional learners: Who needs to know what? *Gifted Child Quarterly,* 57(3), 169-180.

Ford, D. (2011). Closing the achievement gap: Gifted education must join the battle. *Gifted Child Today, 34*(1), 31-34.

Ford, D., Davis, J., & Grantham, T. (2017). *Changing the narrative: Profiles of young black gifted scholars.* Waco, TX: Prufrock Press.

Gilman, B. J. (2008). *Academic advocacy for gifted children: A parent's complete guide* (2nd ed.). Tucson, AZ: Great Potential Press.

Goerss, J. (2011). *Asynchronous development.* Retrieved from http://sengifted.org/asynchronous-development.

Goertzel, V., Goertzel, M. G., Goertzel, T. G., & Hansen, A. M. (2004). *Cradeles of eminence* (2nd ed.). Tucson, AZ: Great Potential Press.

Great Schools Staff. (2010). *IDEA 2004 close up: Evaluation and eligibility for specific learning disabilites.* Retrieved from https://www.greatschools.org/gk/articles/evaluation-and-eligibility-for-specific-learning-disabilities/.

Gurian, M., & Stevens, K. (2007). *The mind of boys: Saving our sons from falling behind in school and life.* San Francisco, CA: Jossey-Bass.

Gurian, M., Stevens, K., Henley, P., & Truman, T. (2011). *Boys and girls learn differently: A guide for teachers and parents.* San Francisco, CA: Jossey-Bass.

Halloran, J. (2018). *The coping skills for kids workbook: Over 75 coping strategies to help kids deal with stress, anxiety, and anger.* Eau Claire, WI: PESI Publishing and Media.

Hanover Research. (2015). *Engaging high achieving students at risk of dropping out.* Retrieved from https://www.gssaweb.org//wp-content/uploads/2016/04/Engaging-High-Achieving-Students-at-Risk-of-Dropping-Out.pdf.

Hoagie's Gifted Education Page. (2002). *Common myths about gifted students.* Retrieved from http://www.hoagiesgifted.org/eric/fact/myths.html.

How to raise a boy: Navigating the world of boys when you're gender nonconforming. (n.d.). Retrieved from https://www.thecut.com/2018/03/navigating-a-world-of-boys-when-youre-gender-nonconforming.html.

Hughes, J., & Hughes, H. (2011). *Through his eyes and through his mother's eyes.* Retrieved from https://www.sengifted.org/post/through-his-eyes-and-through-his-mother-s-eyes.

Isaacson, K., & Fisher, T. (2007). *Intelligent life in the classroom: Smart kids and their teachers.* Tucson, AZ: Great Potential Press.

Johnsen, S. (2011). *Identifying gifted students: A practical guide* (2nd ed.). Waco, TX: Prufrock Press.

Kaufman, S. (2013). *Blurred lines, androgyny and creativity.* Retrieved from https://www.creativitypost.com/article/blurred_lines_androgyny_and_creativity.

Kay, K. (2000). *Uniquely gifted: Identifying and meeting the needs of twice-exceptional students.* Gilsum, NH: Avocus Publishing.

Kerr, B. (2002). *Gender and genius: A keynote speech to the national curriculm networking conference.* Retrieved from https://education.wm.edu/centers/cfge/_documents/resources/articles/gendergenius.pdf.

Kerr, B., & McKay, R. (2014). *Smart girls in the 21st century: Understanding talented girls and women.* Tucson, AZ: Great Potential Press.

Krisel, S. (2016). *The importance of robust state gifted policiies.* Retrieved from https://www.nagc.org/blog/importance-robust-state-gifted-policies.

Machek, G., & Plucker, J. (2003). *Individual intelligence testing and giftedness: A primer for parents.* Retrieved from https://mcgt.net/wp-content/uploads/2011/02/IntelligenceTestingGiftedness.pdf.

Matthews, D., & Foster, J. F. (2004). *Being smart about gifted children: A guidebook for parents and educators.* Tucson, AZ: Great Potential Press.

McLeod, S. (2009). *Jean Piaget.* Retrieved from https://www.simplypsychology.org/piaget.html.

Nash, D. (2001, December). Enter the mentor. *Parenting for High Potential,* 18-21.

National Association for Gifted Children. (2010). *Redefining giftedness for a new century: Shifting the paradigm.* Retrieved from https://www.nagc.org/sites/default/files/Position%20Statement/Redefining%20Giftedness%20for%20a%20New%20Century.pdf.

National association for gifted children. (2019a). *State of states in gifted education.* Retrieved from https://www.nagc.org/2018-2019-state-states-gifted-education.

National Association for Gifted Children. (2019b). *A definition of giftedness that guides best practice.* Retrieved from https://www.nagc.org/sites/default/files/Position%20Statement/Definition%20of%20Giftedness%20%282019%29.pdf.

National Association for Gifted Children. (n.d.-a). *Glossary terms.* Retrieved from http://www.nagc.org/resources-publications/resources/glossary-terms.

National Association for Gifted Children. (n.d.-b). *Tests and assessments.* Retrieved from https://www.nagc.org/resources-publications/gifted-education-practices/identification/tests-assessments.

National Association for Gifted Children. (n.d.-c). *A brief history of gifted and talented education.* Retrieved from https://nagc.org/resources-publications/resources/gifted-education-us/brief-history-gifted-and-talented-education.

National Association for Gifted Children. (n.d.-d). *Gifted education practices.* Retrieved from http://www.nagc.org/resources-publications/gifted-education-practices.

National Association for Gifted Children. (n.d.-e). *Questions and answers about the every student succeeds act (ESSA).* Retrieved from https://www.nagc.org/sites/default/files/Advocacy/Q%2BA%20on%20ESSA%20%28web%29.pdf.

National Center for Education Statistics. (2019a). *Digest of education statistics.* Retrieved from https://nces.ed.gov/programs/digest/d19/.

National Center for Education Statistics. (2019b). *Children and youth with disabilities.* Retrieved from https://nces.ed.gov/programs/coe/pdf/Indicator_CGG/coe_cgg_2019_05.pdf.

National Center for Education Statistics. (2020). *Fast facts: Back to school statistics.* Retrieved from https://nces.ed.gov/fastfacts/display.asp?id=372.

National Education Association. (2006). *The twice-exceptional dilemma.* Retrieved from https://www.nagc.org/sites/default/files/key%20reports/twiceexceptional.pdf.

National Research Center on the Gifted and Talented. (2009). *A meeting of the minds on 2e.* Retrieved from http://www.2enewsletter.com/subscribers_only/arch_symposium_public_7-09.htm.

National Society for the Gifted and Talented. (2018). *Giftedness defined.* Retrieved from https://www.nsgt.org/giftedness-defined/#8.

Neihart, M. (2011). *The impact of giftedness on psychological well-being.* Retrieved from http://sengifted.org/the-impact-of-giftedness-on-psychological-well-being.

Newhall, P. (2012). *Language-based teaching series: Language-based learning disabilities.* Prides Crossing, MA: Landmark Outreach Program.

Office of elementary and secondary education: United States department of education. (n.d.). *Title 1: Improving the academic achievement of the disadvantaged.* Retrieved from https://oese.ed.gov/offices/office-of-formula-grants/school-support-and-accountability/essa-legislation-table-contents/title-i-part-a/.

Ohio Association for Gifted Children. (2018). *Gifted rule and law.* Retrieved from https://oagc.com/gifted-rule-and-law/.

Ohio Department of Education. (2018-a). *Implementing the operating standards for indentifying and serving students who are gifted: A guide for Ohio school distircts and educators.* Retrieved from https://education.ohio.gov/getattachment/Topics/Other-Resources/Gifted-Education/Rules-Regulations-and-Policies-for-Gifted-Educatio/Implementing-the-Operating-Standards-for-Identifying-and-Serving-Students-Who-are-Gifted.pdf.aspx?lang=en-US.

Ohio Department of Education. (2018-b). *Ohio operating standards for identifying and serving students who are gifted.* Retrieved from http://education.ohio.gov/getattachment/Topics/Other-Resources/

Gifted-Education/Rules-Regulations-and-Policies-for-Gifted-Educatio/Ohio-Administrative-Code-3301-51-15.pdf.aspx?lang=en-US.

Ohio Department of Education. (2018-c). *Ohio school report cards data spreadsheets.* Retrieved from http://education.ohio.gov/Topics/Data/Report-Card-Resources.

Ohio Department of Education. (2020). *Gifted indicator.* Retrieved from https://education.ohio.gov/Topics/Other-Resources/Gifted-Education/Reporting/Gifted-Indicator.

Peters, D. (2012). *Coping 101: Building persistence and resilience in gifted children.* Retrieved from https://summitcenter.us/wp-content/uploads/2011/07/Coping-101-GEC_Winter_2012-3.pdf.

Peters, D. (2013). *From worrier to warrior: A guide to conquering your fears.* Goshen, KY: Gifted Unlimited.

Peters, D. (2013). *Make your worrier a warrior: A guide to conquering your child's fears.* Tucson, AZ: Great Potential Press.

Peters, D., Reid, L., & Davis, S. (2020). *The worrier workbook: A guide for conquering your worry monster.* Goshen, KY: Gifted Unlimited.

Pew Research Center. (2013). *A survey of LGTB Americans: Social acceptance.* Retrieved from https://www.pewresearch.org/social-trends/2013/06/13/a-survey-of-lgbt-americans/.

Pollack, W. (1998). *Real boys: Rescuing our sons from the myths of boyhood.* New York: Henry Holt.

Reis, S. M., & Renzulli, J. S. (2009, October). The gifted constitute a single homogeneous group and giftedness is a way of being that stays in the person over time and experiences. *Gifted Child Quarterly, 53*(4), 233-235.

Reis, S., Westburg, K., Kulikowich, J., Calliard, F., Herbert, T., Purcell, J., …Plucker, J. (1992). *Why not let high ability students start school in January? The curriculum compacting study.* Storrs, CT: The University of Connecticut.

Renzulli, J., & Gaesser, A. (2015). *A multi-criteria system for the identification of high achieving and creative/productive/giftedness.* Retrieved from https://gifted.uconn.edu/schoolwide-enrichment-model/high_achieving_creative-productive_giftedness/.

Reuter, T. (2019). *Standing up to OCD workbook for kids: 40 activities to help childern stop unwanted thoughts, control compulsive behaviors, and overcome anxiety.* Emeryville, CA: Rockridge Press.

Reynolds, C. R., & Kamphaus, R. W. (2002). *The clinician's guide to the behavior assessment system for children.* New York: Guilford.

Rief, S. (2016). *How to reach and teach children with ADD/ADHD: Practical techniques, strategies, and interventions.* San Francisco, California: Jossey-Bass.

Rimm, S. (2006). *When gifted students underachieve: What you can do about it.* (F. Karnes, & K. Stephens, Eds.) Waco, TX: Prufrock Press.

Robbins, S. H. (2012). *The everything parent's guide to raising a gifted child.* Avon, MA: Adams Media.

Roberts, J., & Inman, T. (2001, December). Mentoring and your child: Developing a successful relationship. *Parenting for High Potential,* 8-10.

Roeper, A. (1982). *How the gifted cope with their emotions.* Retrieved from http://www.positivedisintegration.com/Roeper1982.pdf.

Rogers, K. B. (2002). *Re-forming gifted education: How parents and teachers can match the program to the child.* Tucson, AZ: Great Potential Press.

Schwartz, K. (2015). *Why kids need to move, touch, and experience to learn.* Retrieved from https://www.kqed.org/mindshift/39684/why-kids-need-to-move-touch-and-experience-to-learn.

Silverman, L. (2009). *What we have learned about gifted children.* Retrieved from https://www.hoagiesgifted.org/we_have_learned.htm.

Streznewski, M. K. (1999). *Gifted grown-ups: The mixed blessings of extraordinary potential.* New York: Wiley.

Supporting Emotional Needs of the Gifted. (n.d.). *SENG misdiagnosis initiative.* Retrieved from https://www.sengifted.org/misdiagnosis-initiative.

Sword, L. (2011). *Emotional intensity in gifted children.* Retrieved from https://www.sengifted.org/post/emotional-intensity-in-gifted-children.

Tomlinson, C. A. (2001). *How to differentiate instruction in mixed ability classrooms* (2nd ed.). Alexandria, VA: Association for Supervision and Curriculum Depvelopment.

Trail, B. (2006). *15 year review: Parenting twice-exceptional children through frustration to success.* Retrieved from https://www.davidsongifted.

org/gifted-blog/15-year-review-parenting-twice-exceptional-children-through-frustration-to-success/.

Tyre, P. (2008). *The trouble with boys: A surprising report card on our sons, their problems at school, and what parents and educators must do.* New York: Crown.

United States Department of Education. (2020-a). *United States department of education fiscal year 2020 budget.* Retrieved from https://www2.ed.gov/about/overview/budget/budget20/summary/20summary.pdf.

United States Department of Education. (2020-b). *Every student succeeds act: A new education law.* Retrieved from https://www2.ed.gov/policy/elsec/leg/essa/index.html.

United States Department of Education. (2021). *Science, technology, engineering, and math, including computer science.* Retrieved from https://www.ed.gov/Stem.

United States Department of Education. (n.d.). *Every student succeeds act (ESSA).* Retrieved from https://www.ed.gov/ESSA/.

United States Department of Education Office for Civil Rights . (2014). *Civil rights data collection: Data snapshots: College and career readiness.* Retrieved from https://www2.ed.gov/about/offices/list/ocr/docs/crdc-college-and-career-readiness-snapshot.pdf.

United States Department of Education Office for Civil Rights. (2012). *Gender equity in education: A snapshot.* Retrieved from https://www2.ed.gov/about/offices/list/ocr/docs/gender-equity-in-education.pdf.

United States Department of Education: Office of Special Education and Rehabilitative Services . (2015). *Memorandum.* Retrieved from https://www2.ed.gov/policy/speced/guid/idea/memosdcltrs/041715osepmemo15-082q2015.pdf.

United States National Commission on Excellence in Education. (1983). *A nation at risk: The imperative for eduational reform: A report to the nation and the Secretary of Education.* Retrieved from https://edreform.com/wp-content/uploads/2013/02/A_Nation_At_Risk_1983.pdf.

University of Washington. (2015). *What is the difference between an IEP and a 504 plan?* Retrieved from https://www.washington.edu/doit/what-difference-between-iep-and-504-plan.

Van Gemert, L. (2017). *Perfectionism: A practical guide to managing "never good enough".* Tucson, AZ: Great Potential Press.

VanTassel-Baska, J. (1998). *Excellence in educating gifted and talented learners.* Denver, CO: Love.

Way, N. (2011). *Deep secrets: Boy's friendships and the crisis of connection.* Cambridge, MA: Harvard University Press.

Webb, J. T., Amend, E. R., Beljan, P., Webb, N. E., Kuzujanakis, M., Olenchak, F. R., & Goerss, J. (2016). *Misdiagnosis and dual dianosis of gifted children and adults: ADHD, bipolar, OCD, Asperger's, depression, and other disorders* (2nd ed.). Tucson, AZ: Great Potential Press.

Webb, J. T., Gore, J. L., Amend, E. R., & Devries, A. R. (2007). *A parent's guide to gifted children.* Tucson, AZ: Great Potential Press.

Wessling, S. (2012). *How other parents add to the challenge of raising gifted kids.* Retrieved from http://sukiwessling.com/2012/07/how-other-parents-add-to-the-challenge-of-raising-gifted-kids/.

Whitmire, R. (2010). *Why boys fail: Saving our sons from an education system that's leaving them behind.* New York: Amacom.

Whitney, C. S., & Hirsch, G. (2007). *A love of learning: Motivation and the gifted child.* Tucson, AZ: Great Potential Press.

Whitney, C. S., & Hirsch, G. (2011). *Helping gifted children soar: A pratical guide for parents and teachers* (2nd ed.). Tucson, AZ: Great Potential Press.

Winebrenner, S. (2003). *Teaching strategies for twice-exceptional students.* Retrieved from http://www.2enewsletter.com/article_strategies_winebrenner.html.

Winebrenner, S., & Brulles, D. (2018). *Teaching gifted kids in today's classroom: Strategies and techniques every teacher can use* (4th ed.). Minneapolis, MN: Free Spirit.

Worrell, F., & Wai, J. (2016). *A nation at risk: How gifted low-income kids are left behind.* Retrieved from https://theconversation.com/a-nation-at-risk-how-gifted-low-income-kids-are-left-behind-56119.

Zakrzewski, V. (2014). *Debunking the myths about boys and emotions.* Retrieved from https://greatergood.berkeley.edu/article/item/debunking_myths_boys_emotions.

Endnotes

1 A good resource for understanding various kinds of 2e conditions can be found in the book, *Misdiagnosis and Dual Diagnoses of Gifted Children and Adults* (2016), by Webb, et al.

2 Cross, 2011

3 Blackburn, 2017

4 For more information, see *Why Boys Fail: Saving Our Sons from an Education System That's Leaving Them Behind* (2010), by Whitmire.

5 National Center for Education Statistics, 2019a

6 Ibid

7 For more information, see *A Parent's Guide to Gifted Children* (2007), by Webb, Gore, Amend, & DeVries, and *Intelligent Life in the Classroom* (2007) by Isaacson & Fisher.

8 Van Gemert, 201)

9 Hanover Research, 2015

10 For more information, see *Changing the Narrative: Profiles of Young, Black Gifted Scholars* (2017), by Ford, Davis, & Grantham, and *A Nation at Risk-How Gifted, Low-Income Kids Are Left Behind*, (2016), by Worrell and Wai

11 Coalition of Schools Educating Boys of Color, 2018

12 See *Smart Boys: Talent, Manhood, and the Search for Meaning*, by Cohn & Kerr, (2001) and *Bright, Talented and Black: A Guide for Families of African American Learners*, by Davis (2010).

13 Cohn & Kerr, 2001

14 Ibid

15 Ibid

16 Tyre, 2008

17 Gurian, Stevens, Henley, & Truman, 2011

18 Ibid

19 National Center for Education Statistics, 2019b

20 Webb, Amend, Beljan, Webb, Kuzujanakis, Olenchak, & Goerss, 2016

21 Pollack, 1998 For more information see *Debunking the myths about boys' emotions* by Zakrzewski (2014)

22 See *Raising boys: Why boys are different and how to help them become happy and well-balanced men* by Biddulph (2013) and *When boys become boys: Developing, relationships and masculinity* by Chu (2014)

23 See *A survey of LGTB Americans: Social and demographic trends* by Pew Research Center (2013) and *Five key findings about LGBT Americans* by Brown (2017)

24 Kerr, 2002

25 Pollack, 1998; For more information see *Deep secrets: Boys' friendships and the crisis of connection* by Way (2011)

26 Deligeorge, 2013

27 See Cohn & Kerr (2011) and Kerr & McKay (2014)

28 For more information on feminine seeming boys getting bullied see: https://www.huffpost.com/entry/ballet-bullying_n_59d5148ce4b0218923e724bf by Angyal, (2017); https://www.thecut.com/2018/03/navigating-a-world-of-boys-when-youre-gender-nonconforming.html, (n.d.)

29 Kaufman, 2013

30 National Association for Gifted Children, n. d.(-a)

31 See more information: *A love for learning* by Whitney and Hirsch (2007) and *When gifted students underachieve: What you can do about it* by Rimm (2006)

32 Hughes and Hughes, 2011

33 United States Department of Education, 2012

34 National Center for Education Statistics, 2020

35 National Education Association, 2006

36 Gilman, 2008

37 National Research Center on the Gifted and Talented, 2009

38 Foley-Nicpon, Assouline, &Colangelo, 2013

39 Baum, Schader, & Owen, 2017

40 National Association for Gifted Children, 2019a

41 National Association for Gifted Children, 2019b

42 Webb, et al., 2016

43 Ibid

44 Great Schools Staff, 2010

45 Center for Parent Resources and Information, 2019

46 Brody & Mills, 1997

47 United States Department of Education: Office of Civil Rights, 2014

48 Unites States Department of Education: Office of Special Education and Rehabilitative Services, 2015

49 Winebrenner, 2003

50 National Association for Gifted Children, n.d.(-b)

51 More detailed explanation of pediatric neuropsychological assessment of gifted children can be found in the book, *Misdiagnosis and Dual Diagnoses of Gifted Children and Adults*, 2nd edition by Webb, et al, 2016

52 Gilman, 2008

53 Carol Dweck (2007), in her book *Mindset*, has clearly demonstrated the importance of how a child views his or her abilities.

54 Colorado Department of Education, 2017

55 Information about these educational options and how to implement them can be found in Karen Rogers (2002) book, *Re-Forming Gifted Education: How Parents and Teachers Can Match the Program to the Child*, in Winebrenner and Brulles (2012), *Teaching Gifted Kids in Today's Classroom: Strategies and Techniques Every Teacher Can* use, 3rd ed., and in Brulles, Brown, and Winebrenner (2016), *Differentiated Lessons for Every Learner: Standards-Based Activities and Extensions for Middle School.*

56 Tomlinson, 2001

57 The importance of deliberate practice is excellently described in See Coyle (2009), *The talent code: Greatness isn't born, It's grown. Here's how.*

58 See Reis, et al, 1992; Rogers, 2002

59 Rogers, 2002

60 Neihart, 2011

61 See Webb, et al, (2016)

62 Fiedler, Lange, & Winebrenner, 2002

63 Ibid

64 See Reis and Renzulli, 2009 as well as Webb, et al, 2016

65 National Association for Gifted Children, n.d.(-c)

66 National Society for the Gifted and Talented, 2018

67 See Rogers (2002) as well as Assouline, et al (2015)

68 National Association for Gifted Children, n.d.(-d)

69 Colangelo & Assouline, & Gross, 2004

70 Assouline, Colangelo, VanTassel-Baska, & Lupkowski-Shiplik, 2015

71 See Beljan, 2011; Davis, 2010; Ford, 2011; and Webb, et al, 2016

72 Fedler, Taradash, Antonie, Ricci, Stemple, & Byamugisha, 2015

73 Renzulli & Gaesser, 2015

74 Berger, 2014

75 Rogers, 2002

76 Trail, B., 2006

77 Ibid; See also Kay, 2000

78 Alvino, 1995, Webb, Gore, Armend & DeVries, 2007

79 Reynolds & Kamphaus, 2002

80 Webb et al., 2016

81 Ibid

82 See Dweck, 2007

83 Reuter, 2019

84 Centers for Disease Control and Prevention, 2021

85 University of Washington, 2015

86 Estroff, n.d.

87 Rief, 2016

88 See *Make your worrier a warrior: A guide to conquering your child's fears* by Peters (2013), *From worrier to warrior: A guide to conquering your fears* by Peters (2013), *The warrior workbook: A guidebook for conquering your worry monster* by Peters (2020)

89 Burruss & Kaenzig, 2011

90 Ibid

91 Cain, 2012

92 Burruss & Kaenzig, 2011

93 For information on teaching relaxation/coping strategies and techniques see *Coping skills for kids' workbook: Over 75 coping strategies to help kids deal with stress, anxiety, and anger* by Halloran (2016)

94 For information about enhancing learning environments see *Creating environments for learning: Birth to age 8*, 3rd ed. By Bullard (2017), *The classroom of choice: Giving students what they need and getting what you* want by Erwin (2004), and *Engagement by design: Creating learning environments where students thrive* by Fisher, Frey, Quaglia, Smith, & Lande (2018).

95 For more information helping children with Executive Function Disorder see *Smart but Scattered* by Dawson & Guare, (2009)

96 For more information about dysgraphia see *Handwriting: Brain-body disconnect: Adaptive teaching techniques to unlock a child's dysgraphia for the classroom and home* by Dotterer (2019)

97 Tomlinson, 2001

98 Wessling, 2012

99 Roeper, 1982

100 American Speech-Language-Hearing Association, n.d.

101 Web, et al., 2016

102 Newhall, 2012

103 Ibid

104 Machek & Plucker, 2003

105 Robbins, 2012

106 Streznewski, 1999

107 Goertzel, Goertzel, Goertzel, & Hansen, 2004

108 Distin, 2006

109 Mathews & Foster, 2004

110 VanTassel-Baska, 1998

111 Roberts & Inman, 2001

112 Nash, 2001

113 Assouline, Colangelo, Lupkowksi-Shoplik, Lipscomb & Forstadt, 2009

114 Webb et al., 2016

115 For more information on multiple assessments to identify gifted students within an increasingly diverse population see *Identifying gifted students: A practical guide* (2nd ed.) by Johnsen, 2011

116 For more information about characteristics of gifted children see https://www.nagc.org/resources-publications/resources/my-child-gifted/common-characteristics-gifted-individuals/traits; Growing up gifted (8th ed.) by Clark, 2013

117 United States National Commission on Excellence in Education, 1983

118 United States Department of Education, 2015

119 National Association for Gifted Children, n.d.(-e)

120 United States Department of Education, 2020 (-a)

121 National Association for Gifted Children, 2019(-a)

122 For information on how Title I funds are allocated for gifted and talented students see United States Department of Education, 2020 (-b); Office of Elementary and Secondary Education, n.d.

123 Ohio Association for Gifted Children, 2018

124 For more information see *Academic advocacy for gifted children: A parent's complete guide*, by Gilman (2008), Re-forming gifted education: *How parents and teachers can match the program to the child*, by Rogers (2002)

125 For more information see *Implementing the operating standards for identifying and serving students who are gifted* by Ohio Department of Education, 2018(-a)

126 For more information see *Ohio operating standards for identifying and serving students who are gifted and talented by* Ohio Department of Education, 2018(-b)

127 For more information see *Ohio* school report cards data spreadsheets by Ohio Department of Education, 2020

128 Ibid

129 See Ohio Department of Education, 2018(-c)

130 Krisel, 2016

131 Augustine & Crew, 2016

132 Sword, 2011

133 Schwartz, 2015

134 McLeod, 2009

135 Gurian & Stevens, 2007

136 "Matthews & Foster, 2004

137 S.T.E.M is curriculum based on the idea of educating students in four specific disciplines—science, technology, engineering, and mathematics-in an interdisciplinary and applied approach. It is relevant for 2e boys because it encompasses the most engaging, hands-on subjects in school. S.T.E.M. education develops skills like communication, problem-solving, critical thinking, and data analysis. See http://www.ed.gov/Stem

138 Silverman, 2009

139 Pollack, 1998

140 Whitney & Hirsch, 2011

141 Peters, 2012; Sword, 2011; Whitney & Hirsch, 2011

About the Author

Deborah (Deb) Gennarelli is currently a gifted education consultant with 40 years of experience as an educator working with diverse student populations in three states. As an educator, Deb has served in numerous roles including curriculum writer, team leader, chair of academic committees and school improvement teams, grant writer, and mentor to first-year teachers.

She is also a professional development speaker on the identification and education of gifted children, twice-exceptional students, and meeting the needs of all students through differentiated studies.

Deb has received three different school districts Teacher of the Year awards, All-County Teaching Team award, and two Ohio GAR Foundation Education Initiative grants for Smart Technology.

She is a member of National Association for Gifted Children (NAGC), Ohio Association for Gifted Children (OAGC), and Supporting Emotional Needs of the Gifted (SENG).

Deb lives in Northeast Ohio with her husband Bob. They enjoy traveling and spending time with their daughter Nicole, son-in-law Noah and grandson Milo.